THE RED DUST OF OB_____

Sunrise Ministries

Working with the rural church in the
United Kingdom and overseas

www.ruralmissions.org.uk

The Red Dust of Obambo

and other stories

Discovering the grace of God in all
the circumstances of life

MONICA COOK

THANKFUL BOOKS
with Sunrise Ministries

Copyright © Monica Cook 2006

First published 2006

Published, in association with Sunrise Ministries,
by Thankful Books c/o P.O. Box 2118, Seaford BN25 9AR

ISBN-13: 978 1 905084 11 1
ISBN-10:   1 905084 11 0

Unless otherwise indicated, Scripture quotations are from the
HOLY BIBLE, NEW INTERNATIONAL VERSION © 1973, 1978, 1984
by the International Bible Society. Used by permission.

Book design and production for the publisher by
Bookprint Creative Services, <www.bookprint.co.uk>
Printed in Great Britain.

Contents

Acknowledgements

A huge thank you to everyone who has been involved with the writing of this book, especially the following:

Chris Henderson who badgered me into writing it.

Anna Brock for ghost-writing the manuscript.

Jeanette Howard for reading the manuscript twice and making helpful suggestions.

Sheila Kemble for proofreading the manuscript.

And to all those who have encouraged me to make a record of my experiences abroad.

Preparation: A Purpose and a Plan

I was born over half a century ago and brought up on a farm in Norfolk. My father, George, managed the farm and my mother Rhoda, was a housewife and auxiliary nurse. I had a younger brother and we grew up enjoying the open air and farm life. The farm was isolated and situated miles from the nearest village. We attended a Brethren Church regularly and received sound, Bible based teaching from an early age.

When I was old enough to go to school I attended the "local" village school which was private. Later my brother joined me there for our half days of education. I had my own bicycle and would cycle the seven miles to school in the morning with my mother, who carried my brother on back of her bike. Mother would then return to the farm, cycling back to meet us three hours later when school ended. I always wondered how my mother kept so fit and healthy and realised in later years that cycling twenty-eight miles a day five days a week probably had a lot to do with it. School, like home life, was idyllic. There were only two classes and we were spoilt and not stretched much at all. I remember one of the teachers had a sister who was ill in bed. This sister loved having visitors and liked to talk to the pupils. On one visit with my brother,

I took along one of my dolls who unfortunately had no clothes. I was very shy at the time and struggled to make conversation. My teacher's sister must have been busy over the next few days, for when I went to see her again she had made a set of clothes for my doll.

When I turned seven years of age, my brother and I were sent to a Catholic school. We had to catch the train every day and I didn't really like the new school at all. The nuns were very strict which didn't suit my free spirit. Each day I was given a list of spellings to learn but I never bothered. To this day I don't know why. Having been used to half days at the private village school perhaps I felt the school days was long enough. Why do school work in my free time? And I didn't learn that it was wrong not to practise these spellings as every day I failed my spelling test and was kept in at break times. The more the nuns told me off, the more stubborn I became.

At home, on the farm, I rode as much as possible, loving to look after the horses and enjoying the fresh air. I spent as much time as possible outside, helping on the farm. My brother and I drove tractors from an early age and were included in the running of the farm. We used to take it in turns to drive the tractors. For instance one of us would drive a tractor out into the fields to the cattle. Whilst one was driving, the other would throw the cattle feed to the ground. Sharing tasks like this meant more time to ourselves! I remember harvest time when everyone helped to bring the crops in. The sun always seemed to shine and we would work late into the evenings. I would drive a tractor out with an empty cart on the back. The harvesters would pile the cut corn, stalks and all into my cart until it was full. Then I would drive the cart to where the corn would be stacked and other farmhands would start unloading it. Meanwhile my brother would drive up in his tractor with an empty cart which would be connected to my tractor and back I drove to the harvesters to repeat the process all over again. I couldn't bear to miss anything and often my mother would find me asleep outside. To be honest, I am still like that! I cannot bear to miss anything exciting that is going on and will deprive myself of sleep until the event is over.

I was conscious, even as a small child that my mother prayed for me regularly and when I was about ten years old I realised that my parents' faith was not my own. I remember standing in the farmyard when I discovered that I could not depend on my parents' faith to save myself. There and then I prayed a short prayer, dedicating my life to Jesus Christ and believe that at that moment I became a Christian.

I was sent away to boarding school when I was thirteen years old and loved every minute of it. I was a termly boarder at Wymondham College which had 800 boarders and was a mixed sex school. Although I enjoyed my time at boarding school my faith didn't develop at all. I was doing all the things I knew a good Christian should do such as praying and reading my Bible daily. (Once I lost my Bible and couldn't read it for weeks. I never owned up to losing it as I thought people might think I'd lose my faith). I had to go to church as my mother had signed the right form – so there was no getting out of that. I also attended the Christian Union meetings regularly, but I didn't learn how to be a Christian during this time, I was just going through the motions, thinking that that was what a Christian did. I do remember one prayer I made during this time at Wymondham College. I think it may have been when we were asked to think about what career we wanted in life, so I would have been aged between sixteen and eighteen. I remember telling God that I'd do absolutely anything for Him, but begged Him not to send me abroad. The idea of working overseas absolutely petrified me.

In the last couple of years at Wymondham College we worked towards either the career we had chosen or took exams to go on to further education. My father wanted me to work for the milk marketing board. My mother, however, wished me to become an auxiliary nurse. All I wanted to do was become a teacher. I had wanted to be a teacher for years and I believe now that God put that desire in my heart. I followed my inner promptings and went to Bishop Grossteste College in Lincoln to qualify as a teacher.

I was eighteen when I started my teacher training and from that age God took hold of me and started changing me. I had no idea how revolutionary going to college would be. I was put into a room on campus with three other girls, one of whom was a Christian. Looking back I can see that God had his hand on me the whole time, guiding me to the right people and making sure that I was in the right place at the right time for his purposes. Through this Christian girl I met up with other Christians at the college and accompanied them to the Thomas Cooper Memorial Church, abandoning my Brethren roots without a second thought. (Though I did not abandon the Brethren teaching that had been instilled into me over the years). At the TCM Church I was introduced to Dr Lechler and his wife who invited a group of us round for tea. I was quite shocked at the conversation over tea and cake. The Doctor and his wife expected us to be witnessing to others about our faith and to start up a Christian Union at the college. The other Christians with me were all eager to witness and not wanting anyone to know that I'd never been involved with anything like this, I eagerly joined in too.

Talking about my faith was a bit intimidating at first but soon got easier the more I did it. I also found that I began to have a real relationship with Jesus, and my faith developed and grew. We were successful in launching a Christian Union and often invited Dr Lechler to come and speak at the meetings. We held special events and met every day after breakfast to pray together. Dr Lechler and his wife were invaluable in their support of us and we would meet with them a couple of times a week as well as attending Bible studies run by the Doctor. I also got involved with a Sunday School at another church in Lincoln and my faith was recognised by both lecturers and students. Many people became Christians during the three years I was at Bishop Grossteste College and the work I did there would prove excellent training for my future. I learnt afterwards that many of my student contacts became Christians later on in life and that they had never forgotten my input at college.

When I left college I had to find myself a teaching job as I was now qualified to teach all subjects to 9–13 year olds. In those days you had to apply to the County and if the County accepted you, they decided where you would teach first. The County didn't like you to work too near your home so they would give you a post many miles from your home village so you would have to move out and become part of a different community. I think the theory behind it was that you would become too comfortable living at home and would never move on. Even back then you were expected to work your way up the teaching ladder. I applied to Norfolk County Council and they gave me a job seventy miles from my home farm in a village called Marham RAF. I didn't know until the Friday before I started where I would be teaching and until I walked in to the school on the Tuesday morning I had no idea who or what I would be teaching.

It was a bit of a shock therefore to discover that I was to teach a class of forty reception pupils. I had no experience of that age group at all. Although this was a village school, the classes were large and the reception class totalled eighty-four pupils. The other forty-four pupils were taught by another teacher who took me under her wing right from the start. We shared one room and our separate classes had their backs to each other but the noise took a bit of getting used to. My fellow teacher was in her forties and had a lot of experience of working with young children. We would combine our work load, for instance I would take the bright pupils from both classes for maths, whilst the other teacher took the ones who were good at English. We also took it in turns to read the whole class a story at the end of the day whilst the other tidied up and prepared things for the next day. I learnt a lot in the year that we worked together and discovered that I enjoyed working with smaller children as well as older ones.

At the beginning of my second year in Marham RAF, the teacher who had given me so much support and help left, as her husband (who was in the RAF) was posted abroad. She was replaced by Margaret MacDonald who was a Catholic and very enthusiastic about her beliefs. Margaret had six children under eleven years of age and was often overwhelmed by everything she had to do both at home and at school. Having been supported by Margaret's predecessor, I now had the experience of supporting and looking after Margaret. During my second year of teaching I began to get involved with other organisations. I trained as a local preacher in the Methodist Church, became a Guider and ran a Brownie pack. I also took part in a camping course for Guides and Brownies and gained a qualification which enabled me to take packs away for camping holidays.

Although I kept to the curriculum at school, the children knew I was a Christian. In later years I met up with one boy who had been taught by me when five or six. I met him at a church service I'd been involved in and he was now in his early twenties and eager to tell me that he'd become a Christian. He mentioned that he knew I had been a Christian when I had taught him.

I had known a local young man for many years and considered us to be close friends. I had always thought that this friendship might lead to marriage. But in the years after leaving college, God gradually impressed on me that marriage at that time wasn't right for me and that he had a different plan for my life. So I gave up all thoughts of relationships and marriage and threw myself into work and outside activities.

Time passed quickly and I applied for my second teaching post and moved to another school in the Norfolk area. As I had enjoyed teaching reception pupils so much I applied for an infant post and lived at home all the time I worked at this new school. I became extremely busy as the more I did, the more people praised me and thought well of me. I taught in the school five days a week, ran a Sunday School, a Youth Club, a Children's Club in another village and a Brownie pack, was church treasurer and a local preacher. I also looked after five children whose father suffered from depression. When he went into one of his depressive bouts he couldn't bear to have the children in the house so I used to take them to the seaside or out for walks. I was asked to attend children's birthday parties many times as parents recognised me as someone interested in children. I also ran a football team in my home village. The boys were keen on football and formed a team which I organised. I held several practices for them during the week and every Saturday we would go and play a match and lose miserably. I had no idea how football was to be played and just made sure they didn't fight during the practice sessions. The boys loved being able to be on a team though! Sometimes, on a summer evening I would pick up any school children who wanted to go out and take them to the beach. We'd take along a small picnic and play games on beach and then I'd take them home. I was in my twenties at the time and seemed to have boundless energy. In all my busyness there was a niggling thought that even though everyone around me thought I was wonderful, God didn't think that at all. I was rushing all the time. I prepared sermons and teaching notes, but I didn't have time to pray properly or read my Bible regularly. I knew Jesus was my saviour but he certainly was not Lord of my life.

Suddenly, amidst all this busyness, I had a strong desire to go to Australia. At that time I had the chance of going on a teaching exchange to Australia and it would certainly stand me in good stead for promotion and to work my way up the teaching career ladder. Two thousand teachers applied to go to Australia on this exchange. I appeared before panels and attended interviews and even travelled to London to be approved. I didn't think I'd have much chance, not with 1,999 other applicants. But I believe now that God put the desire for Australia in my heart and he made sure I did well in all my interviews. Finally, thirty teachers were chosen for the exchange and I was amongst them.

I gave up all my commitments and took the boat to Australia. For six and half weeks I had nothing to do and realised how busy I had been. My relationship with Jesus was restored and I made many friends amongst the teachers travelling with me to Australia. Several of the friends I made on the trip to Australia have stayed friends over the years and support me now in my current work. I enjoyed every moment of my time in Australia – both the teaching and the social life. As I wasn't rushing around I had more time to hear what God was saying to me and with a mixture of excitement and trepidation I realised He was calling me to live by faith and be available to do what He wanted me to do.

When I returned from my stint in Australia I was offered a deputy headship but refused it. To the shock of everyone around me I gave up teaching and a lucrative career and announced that I was going to Bible College to train officially for some kind of Christian work. A non-believing couple in my home village just couldn't understand why I was doing such a foolish thing and quite despaired of me. They have since become Christians and now understand why I did what I did. Living by faith was a lot harder than I had imagined. I couldn't get a grant to live on whilst I studied. The Methodist Church I was attending had the grand sum of six members, one of whom was me. So I knew I couldn't expect any financial help from the church. I applied to the Birmingham Bible Institute as that felt right. I got through the interview and was offered a place but when I discovered how high the fees were I couldn't see how I'd be able to afford them. I then decided that I would go to the New Life College in London and study in the evenings. Apparently teachers were desperately needed in London and I could teach during the day and earn enough money to pay for my fees. I was offered a position at New Life College but told to pray about it for a fortnight before I accepted. I prayed for a whole month hoping God would change His mind. He didn't. So I went back to Birmingham Bible Institute, cap in hand, and asked to be considered again. I was accepted and God provided every penny I needed for the entire two years that I spent there.

To begin with I gave up my pension rights which started me off at college. I found that if I trusted God he provided me with everything I needed, just when I needed it. People told me that I should give up my Mini but I didn't feel that that was right at all and throughout the two years I was able to keep the car roadworthy and running. Someone had drawn a flower on the back of the Mini and it was very popular with the other students. Fellow students learnt to drive in it and I was often required to transport people to CU meetings and events.

I did not get on well at the Institute initially. I was a free spirit and very independent. I had been a teacher and knew how to organise my time. However, at the Institute we were told when to get up, when to spend time reading the Bible, when to pray and we even had supervised study which really rankled. My pride got the better of me for the first few days and I rebelled against everything. Then, during a time of prayer, I realised that if God had put me here I needed to accept things as they were. After that my time at the Institute was good fun and taught me lot about sharing Christianity and prayer, rather than teaching me anything academic. God even gave me back my responsibilities at one point and I became head girl for a time!

One weekend I had planned to go home but only had a small amount of petrol in my tank. I knew it wouldn't be enough for the 200 mile journey between Birmingham and

Norfolk but I felt God telling me I should go and to trust him. So I obediently set off, keeping my eye on the petrol indicator. As the needle slowly dropped I wondered how far I'd get before I ran out completely. I had reached the Huntingdon area when I heard God telling me to go into the nearest petrol station and fill up with petrol. I had very little money with me, certainly not enough to pay for a full tank. Nervously I began filling up and looked across at the man at the pump next to me. Perhaps I just looked like a poor student. Perhaps the man was just the generous sort. Whatever the cause, God had put him there at that time and he paid for my petrol!

One of the big questions that hung over me all the time I was there was – what does God want me to do once I've finished training? My experience so far in life had been in children's and rural work. When someone from the Rural Society came to speak to us at the college, I went along to hear him. The speaker talked about all the different kinds of work they did for quite a while. When he asked for questions, a girl nearby put her hand up and asked; "What opportunities are there for women?"

"Oh, we fit them in!" smiled the speaker tolerantly. I felt a flash of anger at the speaker's condescension. "If they were the last people on earth, I wouldn't join them!" I announced firmly to those around me. "I will not be 'fitted in'!"

Part of the college course required students to be involved in some kind of mission. I was looking around for a mission to join when I discovered that the Rural Society were asking for a group of students to help with a mission they were running at Malmesbury. Although I wasn't keen on the Rural Society, not after the speaker's comment about women, I thought it would be good experience for me – I had to help some Christian organisation anyway. The mission would be running for two weeks and I went along daily to help out. By the end of the two weeks I knew that this was where God wanted me to be and had to swallow my angry words I'd uttered previously. The director of the Rural Society asked me to join them after college and that was all the confirmation I needed.

When I began working for the Rural Society in the 1970s I looked back over the years and realised that everything I'd been through and done had prepared me for the work I was now doing. God clearly showed me that the work I was to concentrate on was village work and children's work. My background in a village environment and my subsequent teaching of young children had prepared me perfectly for the things I was about to be involved in. I realised that God had a purpose for my life and that everything I had been involved in previously had prepared me for the path God had chosen for me. I also discovered that by staying single I was free to do all the travelling that a married woman with children would not have been able to do. Although I was quite happy to be single, I knew that if God wanted me to marry He would bring along the right man at the right time.

I was still living by faith – that was one of the requirements of working for the Rural Society – and I experienced again and again God's provision in times of need. I was involved in children's evangelism and follow-up clubs and travelled nation-wide to various villages holding events throughout the year.

When I joined the Rural Society I still had my Mini that had been with me through college. The car lasted some years and in the 1980s went in for repairs at the Broad Oak garage as I was living in the Brede area. I was told by the garage that the sub-frame had gone and it was going to cost more than I could afford. The organisers of the Rural Society suggested I took the Mini over to a garage in Egerton which was owned by some Christians who supported the Society's work. Phil Oliver owned the garage at Egerton and he and his wife had supported me once when I had been very ill. I had stayed in contact with them through the years and dutifully took the car over to Phil at Easter and felt it was right to ask him to repair the sub-frame, even though I had no money to pay him.

At that time my food and drink was supplied and I was given £4 pocket money a week. I was involved in a team holding some events at Phil's local church that Easter and after the Sunday morning service he approached me. "Your car will be ready next weekend," he told me. "And you won't have to pay for it!" I thought I'd misheard him but Phil insisted it was all sorted out but he wouldn't tell me why the repairs were free.

Later that year, in September I visited some friends and as I walked into their house I just knew that they had had something to do with the repairs to my Mini. So, I risked being rude and asked them if they had been involved with the repairs for my car at Easter. "I had a dream one night," my friend's husband admitted. "I dreamt there was something wrong with your car and felt that God wanted me to do something about it. So the next morning I rang the Rural Society who told me that your car was in Phil's garage. I rang Phil and told him I'd either pay for the repairs or buy you a second-hand car to replace your Mini if it was irreparable."

Phil retired and left the Rural Society and I didn't see him for years. Eventually I heard that he was ill and I really wanted to visit him. I had a visit planned to Egerton to assist in some church events and I wondered if I could combine that with a visit to Phil. I rang Phil's son who said it would be fine to see him and we arranged I'd call in at 6.30 pm one evening. I didn't want to stay too long as Phil was quite poorly but when I walked in I knew I was right to have visited him. Phil was sitting there all radiant – it was like meeting Jesus. We talked about all kinds of things and caught up on news together. Two weeks later he was dead. Afterwards his sister-in-law told me that something I had said to Phil in our conversation had healed a problem in Phil's past. It hadn't been anything to do with me but I felt very humbled at how God had used me in this matter. Apparently after I had gone, Phil said to his sister-in-law "Now I can die in peace."

During the time I was at the Rural Society there was a petrol strike and petrol was rationed. One could only buy one gallon of petrol at a time which made travelling quite difficult for me. I remember travelling out of Hastings and driving up Sedlescombe Road North in order to go home to Brede when I ran out of petrol and had to stop. Wondering what I was going to do, I got out of the car and stared around. At that moment a man came out of a nearby house and asked me what was wrong. I told him I'd run out of petrol and he said to wait a moment and disappeared inside his house. A few minutes later he returned carrying a five-gallon can of petrol. This was poured into my petrol tank and he refused to take any money for it. I have no idea whether he was an angel or just someone whose heart God had moved to help me. I never saw him again but I was able to get safely home that day and didn't need to visit a petrol station for a few days.

Several times I returned to my home village in Norfolk whilst working for the Rural Society. I held missions and meetings and many people came to hear me speak because of the things I'd done for them in the past. Children I had helped with homework and family problems were now grown up and brought their own children along to hear me. It was at this point that I really understood James 2:18, "I will show you my faith by what I do."

When my Mini was finally consigned to the scrap heap I had to share the pool cars allocated to employees of the Rural Society in our area. Once, I drove up to the Garw Valley in Wales in one of the pool cars. I wasn't used to driving this particular car and it wasn't running very well. I was organising a holiday club for school children and the church hall was at the opposite end of the valley to Bridgend where I was staying. I decided to take the bus from Bridgend to the hall as I wasn't keen on breaking down on the Welsh roads. I caught a bus up to the church hall and was totally oblivious to the bus drivers going on strike during the day. When the club had finished I stood at the bus stop and waited and waited. I prayed that God would send a bus soon and eventually a school bus drew up beside me. There was no-one on it and the driver asked me where I wanted to go. I told him where I staying and was driven right to the door of my lodgings! My journey was free, I wasn't required to pay my fare at all!

I travelled back from the Garw Valley on the Sunday to Hastings. At the time I didn't like using a petrol station on a Sunday so I had arranged with some friends in Wiltshire to have some petrol ready for me when I called in to see them at teatime. (The journey was too long to drive on one tank of petrol.) I duly called upon my friends who filled the petrol tank up for me and gave me a five-gallon can to put in the back of the car. I had tea with them and set off again. When I reached the Sutton area of London I decided to top up my petrol tank with the five-gallons in the boot of the car. I took the key out of the ignition and went around to the boot. (The same key was used for both the ignition and the boot.) I unlocked the boot and the key barrel snapped in half. I held the top half in my hand and stared at the other half stuck in the boot lock. What was I to do now? I prayed silently for help and it came into my head to ring the AA. In those days I didn't have a mobile phone so I decided to ask to use the telephone in one of the nearby houses. I started to walk up the nearest path but felt God telling me that this wasn't the right house. So I turned round and took the next path. The people in that house were very sympathetic and let me use their phone. The AA man arrived shortly after my phone call and looked at the key and the lock. He told me that it would be too dangerous to start the car and try and drive it, did I have a spare key? Of course I did, but it was at home, in Brede.

The AA man went away and I asked to use the telephone again. I called my colleague Barry who lived in Hastings and asked him to drive up to Sutton with the spare key. While I waited for him the people whose house I had invaded cooked me a meal and when Barry and his wife Doreen arrived, they cooked them a meal as well! I talked to the people for ages and discovered that their daughter had been one of the teachers I had known on my Australian exchange! They couldn't understand why I had given up a good career for such a precarious way of living now and asked to be sent information on my work with the Rural Society.

A couple of years later I was driving the same car back from Cornwall where I had been training and teaching. I was driving by myself with a lot of equipment on the passenger seat and in the back of the car as well. It was pouring with rain and the windscreen wipers weren't working properly. Near Plymouth I came across a series of sharp bends in the road. Taking the first corner too quickly and I discovered that the equipment in the car was distributed unevenly. The car spun round, hit the side of the road and flipped onto its roof.

My car was blocking the road and before long a great queue of traffic tailed back behind me. I was sitting there a bit surprised, but otherwise all right. Some men got out of their cars and turned my car up the right way. Thanking them I started the car and drove off. Before long I realised what could have happened and turned towards Exeter in order to stay with some friends while I recovered from the shock.

One bank holiday Monday I was taking some information over to Barry who now lived in Herstmonceux. I drove via Catsfield and came out of Church Road near the school in order to turn left. To this day I don't know how the accident happened. Someone in another car was waiting to turn right into Skinners Lane and I managed to plough into the back of this car. All I could do was keep apologising and everyone around me kept telling me to shut up and stop admitting it was my fault. The car I'd been driving was a write-off and I was a bit bruised and in a state of shock. The vehicle I'd crashed into was damaged but not a write-off and I knew the man driving it. The car I'd damaged was his favourite car and he'd owned it for years. The owner was an acquaintance and I didn't know him well. I felt very ashamed at my carelessness as the man had whiplash. We were both taken to hospital for treatment.

My car had been giving me trouble but as it was a write-off I got the insurance money for it. The man in the other car was a Christian and refused to prosecute me which I felt very unworthy about. I didn't even get a point on my licence! He also arranged with friends to loan me a car until I got a new one sorted out and forgave me for damaging his favourite car. With the insurance money I was able to buy a better car that lasted for several years. I was very grateful for the gracious attitude that the injured man had towards me and it taught me a lot about grace and forgiveness. The ironic thing was that a few days after the accident a friend was caught by a police speed camera and fined for doing thirty four mph in a thirty mph limit!

In the mid-nineties I was living in Battle and attending Battle Baptist Church regularly. The church needed someone to co-ordinate the children's and youth work and it soon became evident that I should have a hand in it. In 1997 I took on a part-time role at the church, working sixteen hours a week on top of the village work I was continuing to do. This meant I was more home-based and not travelling quite as extensively as I had been. Just after I started working for the church, my mother, whose health hadn't been good, deteriorated rapidly. As I was more home-based at this time it meant that I could visit her more often until she died in 2000. My hip, which had been giving me trouble for a few years also became worse and it was necessary for me to have a hip replacement in December 2000. During my recuperation period I had more time to rest and felt God was telling me to give up work at the church as he had other plans for my life. When I started asking him what these plans were, He showed me that He wanted me to start working in other countries with children and village work. Once I had recovered from my

operation, I gave up the part-time work at church and immediately invitations from around the world started coming in. I
realised now that I was physically able to travel extensively
once again and that I was also free from any family ties. Seeing
as I had never married, I was free to travel for prolonged
periods of time abroad. Once the invitations started coming
in there was no looking back. I did not need to look for work
abroad, it was already there, waiting for me.

Despite travelling abroad, I still had a lot of work in the UK
which required me to have a good car to carry equipment and
take me all over the country. In 2004 I was still driving a
Sierra 2.3 which I felt very comfortable with and was just
right for the work I was doing. However, I had done over
200,000 miles in it and rust was eating away the bodywork.
I knew it wouldn't get through its MOT in December and was
starting to think about what I should do as I didn't have
enough money as usual for everything. Out of the blue a
friend rang me in June 2004 and said that he felt God was
telling him to buy me another vehicle. (Apparently he had put
some money in a fund which had grown with interest and he
had been asking God what he should do with the money.) The
total sum came to £7,500. That telephone call took place one
evening and the next morning I woke up and thought I'd
dreamt it all.

I began to study cars. I needed something that was large
enough for all my equipment, economical to run and easy on
repairs, but powerful enough to take me all over the country.
I prayed about it and read up about cars and decided on an
Octavia 1.9 Tdi, not really knowing what it was. It just
seemed right to me. I went over to the garage at Bexhill and
saw a car on the forecourt and thought – that's mine! It was
priced at £7,999 and it was an Octavia 1.9 Tdi. I really felt
that this was the right car for me but didn't say anything to
the salesman at the garage. I explained my requirements and
the salesman pointed out the Octavia on the forecourt and

suggested I take it for a test drive. This I did which confirmed my thoughts that this really was the right car for me.

However, I didn't want to make a decision by myself plus the price was a bit too expensive! So I asked my colleague Barry, and Richard the guy who kept my cars running, to have a look at the Octavia for me. Both were very busy and a whole month went by and still they hadn't checked it out for me. Eventually I drove past the Bexhill garage and sadly my Octavia was no longer on the forecourt. I rang Barry and told him it had gone so he agreed to go with me to the garage on the following Monday to sort out another car for me. When we got there on Monday I discovered the Octavia was still there – it had just been moved to the back of the garage. Barry approved of it and the next day Richard went along to see it. He got the price down to £7,500 and another friend, Esther, checked for any serious problems with the Octavia on the internet. To my relief there was nothing that would go seriously wrong with the car. Amazingly, that Octavia 1.9 Tdi was the only one for sale in the whole country. At that point I knew once again that God was with me in every situation and that He was working out the plan He had for my life.

Relationships I have built in the past, even when I was a nominal Christian at boarding school and a too-busy Christian in my first years of teaching, have lasted and continued through to the present day. Many of these people now support my work and without their prayer and financial gifts I could not survive. God has been very gracious to me, using me even when I wasn't listening to Him properly and providing for me at every step. I have learnt to trust God to provide all my needs and to not be so busy that I can't hear what He is saying to me. I intend to continue in the work I am doing until God tells me to stop.

The Red Dust of Obambo

NAIROBI AIRPORT

"I will be with you wherever you go." (Joshua 1:9)

As the aeroplane descended in a wide arc towards Nairobi airport, the ground below appeared as shimmering water. I blinked, blinded by the light, letting my eyes readjust. I knew that the scrubland was brown on the edge of Nairobi and couldn't reconcile this glittering vision with what I had seen on my previous visits. As we drew closer I saw the thousands of tin roofs that make up the slums of Nairobi, covered in water from a downpour during the night. The rising sun was reflected from this shining surface in a dazzling display of light. As the aeroplane touched down, I thought that so often I saw just the tin shacks and the dry dust, but God sees the whole picture – he sees the sun and how it reflects off the roofs. I was determined to keep that picture in mind as I travelled in Kenya this time.

I had first visited Kenya in 1995 and travelled there again in 1997. The purposes of my visits to Kenya were to take both teaching and money. I had concentrated on Obambo village, taking steps to provide them with a clean water supply and raising funds to purchase goats and oxen so that the community could earn money themselves. I had also been finding sponsors for the children there so that their education could be paid for.

In the early days of my contact with Obambo, I had wondered whether to create an Obambo Trust fund. However, there was so much red tape attached to bank accounts in Kenya that it simply was not possible. Instead, my contact in Obambo, Pastor Jack, opened his own bank account and money raised in the UK was transferred bank to bank for safety. Pastor Jack was accountable for his spending to Rural Sunrise who expected receipts for everything he bought.

It was Thursday, 12th April 2001 and for this trip, Battle Baptist – my home church – had given £500 as part of their tithe, which had already been transferred to Pastor Jack's bank. This sum of money had been given specifically by the church in order for the Obambo Christians to erect a church building.

As the aeroplane taxied to a halt I was aware of the excitement rising inside me even as I felt tense. I was back in Kenya where I had longed to be! Everyone unfastened their seat belts and reached for their hand luggage as the disembarkation took place. I checked I had everything with me, including my paper tissues that I carried everywhere. I thought briefly about discarding the old paper hankies in my pocket but decided I didn't have time.

Even though I was expecting it, I still wasn't prepared for the intense heat. It was like walking out into an oven after the air-conditioned aeroplane. Passing through customs was no problem at all and I got £300 cash changed into Kenyan shillings before picking up my luggage from the carousel. With excitement bubbling inside me, I made my way outside the airport.

The first thing that struck me was the sound of a crowd of Kenyans all shouting and trying to attract my attention. They offered taxis and luggage carrying services and I stared in dismay at the sea of round, black faces. I didn't recognise a single person and they all looked the same to me. Then I saw a face I knew at the back of the crowd. Pastor Jack paused to wave at me and then carried on pushing his way through the people. Behind him were eleven other men who were my reception committee. I was used to this by now – although initially on my first trip I had found it strange. The Kenyans were strong on hospitality and to show their appreciation of people visiting them, they turned up in large groups to welcome visitors.

The crowd before me was still clamouring for my attention, trying to earn money from this "rich" white woman as they thought me to be. I stood still, with my luggage in front of me, keeping a look out for pickpockets. When Pastor Jack and the other Kenyans reached me, there were handshakes all round – I had learnt early on that this was the way of greeting visitors in the Obambo community. As I chatted with Pastor Jack, I was aware of the other men moving into position around me, making a protective ring. This had been rather intimidating at first but I knew that this was my friends' way of protecting me against thieves.

We were by now, part of the noisy crowd of Kenyans vying for tourists and businessmen's attentions. I was surrounded by a mass of black bodies and Pastor Jack and I had to shout to each other in order to be heard. Suddenly someone slammed into my back and I stumbled forwards. I would have fallen if Pastor Jack had not caught me and was slightly winded. The shouting grew louder and some of it was angry. I turned round to see one man scrabbling on the ground between people's legs, another man with a clenched fist shouting continuously and a third man, one of my welcoming committee, talking to Pastor Jack very quickly.

On Pastor Jack's orders his friends moved me and my luggage out of the crowd and Jack sent one of them off to find a car. He then explained what had happened. As his friends were forming a ring around me, I had been approached by a thief who had stolen the contents of my cardigan pocket. One of Pastor Jack's friends had seen this happen and caught hold of the thief. Another man in the crowd had seen the pickpocket apprehended and punched him in the face, sending the thief staggering back into me. I felt quite sorry for the pickpocket really. All he'd managed to steal were my dirty paper handkerchiefs!

As I stood there thinking about how Pastor Jack and his friends had protected me, I was reminded of a passage in the

Old Testament. I repeated to myself the verse from Exodus 14:19, "Then the angel of God, who had been travelling in front of Israel's army, withdrew and went behind them." I knew I could be sure that God was with me in every situation, protecting me. The noise of the crowd nearby still filled the air and I thought how the world clamoured for my attention all the time. I reminded myself that the Evil One was roaring around, seeking to devour. I recalled the sensation of falling in the crowd, that helpless feeling, and being rescued and supported by Pastor Jack's arm. I knew that whenever I fell, God would be there to catch me and move me to a place of safety.

We waited and waited in the increasing heat and still Pastor Jack's friend did not arrive with a car. It seemed a long time to me as I was tired from the flight, and after half an hour the car still had not appeared. It was then that I glanced down at my luggage and saw that my main suitcase was fastened with a pink lock. The inner excitement which had been flagging due to the long, hot wait, dispersed in a sinking sensation of horror. This was not my suitcase. I had never owned a pink coloured padlock in my life!

"Jack!" I said, trying not to sound too distraught, "I've got the wrong suitcase! I'm going back into the airport."

Pastor Jack nodded and I left the rest of my luggage with him. The Kenyan natives were not allowed in the airport itself so I had to go back in on my own and returned to the carousel from which I had blithely taken the wrong case less than an hour before. I came across a white couple and an airport official and with them was my case. The woman looked at me as I approached and her face lit up.

"I'm really sorry," I said hastily, putting the suitcase with the pink lock on the floor. "But I picked up your case instead of mine. It's so similar but I've just noticed the pink lock!"

"That's OK!" the woman said with relief as her husband frowned at me. "We were hoping you'd notice when you got to your hotel!"

I smiled and refrained from telling her I wasn't staying in a hotel. The airport official didn't look particularly pleased. The couple had just signed a form saying they'd lost their luggage so I suppose the official thought it a waste of paper! I retrieved my suitcase and returned outside to where Pastor Jack and his friends were waiting beside a car for me.

As we packed ourselves into the car along with my luggage, I reflected that it hadn't been the most auspicious start to my third visit to Kenya. I reminded myself of the view I'd seen of the shimmering water as the aeroplane had come into Nairobi airport and knew that whatever happened, God could see the bigger picture. With that thought in my head, I relaxed a little as the men around me started singing.

NAIROBI SLUMS

Nairobi City is surrounded by satellite slums. These slums have grown up over the years as people have migrated from the remote villages in the countryside in order to find work. The slums consist of thousands of tin shacks and no sanitation. Each tribe seems to concentrate in its own particular area. This was not planned, it just happened, and I was being driven to the area where those from the Luo tribe lived. The Luo tribe come from the Nyanza area in North West Kenya, near Lake Victoria where Obambo is located and where Pastor Jack lives. The people from Obambo who move to Nairobi and work there, send the money they earn back to their families in the villages and twice a year at Easter and Christmas as many as possible return to their family village.

We were on our way to Jack's brother's "house" in one of the Nairobi slums. Between the songs in the car, the men spoke of how they looked forward to seeing their relations at home again and I discovered that a fair number of them would be accompanying Pastor Jack and me to Obambo. The taxi stopped near Sylvester's home and we got out. What hit me first was the smell – it was a pungent, sewer-like stench that invaded my nostrils and mouth. Then I noticed the heat – intense and stifling.

Pastor Jack's brother, Sylvester, was not in but his brother's wife was there along with their four daughters aged ten, seven, six and one. Inside the hut was nothing but a cement floor and a curtain which divided the room into two areas – one for eating and one for sleeping. My luggage was placed behind the curtains on a mattress. Someone went to buy some food and I asked if I could use the toilet. Jack showed me the communal toilet which was situated across the yard.

The heat was almost unbearable, like a great, heavy weight on my head and shoulders. Inside the brick hut there was no air and the place stank. The toilet was just a hole in the ground and as I closed the wooden door behind me I thought that something moved deep in the hole. Swallowing hard I tried to ignore this phenomenon as I really did need the toilet. On my way out of the hut I noticed that the door did not fit the door-frame particularly well, and, as the sun was high, I thought perhaps that it had been a mixture of sunlight and shadows playing across the hole so that it appeared something was moving. As I walked back to the house, under the watchful eye of Pastor Jack who had waited at a discreet distance for me, I recalled my first trip to Kenya and an unfortunate incident with a toilet.

I had been visiting five villages on the Ugandan border and we had spent the night at Busia. Early in the morning I woke after a restless night's sleep due to the humidity and decided to use the toilet before anyone else was awake. I slipped out of the hut we were all sleeping in and made my way down the field to the solitary toilet for the entire compound. This toilet was very modern, I thought as I stepped inside. In the growing light I could see that the floor had been covered with cement, instead of being left as compacted soil. I felt a lot safer in this hut than I had done since I'd left the aeroplane. The walls and roof of the toilet were the usual wattle and dung and I let my mind drift to what I would be speaking on that day.

As I finished and straightened up I heard a loud crack. Glancing down I saw a hairline fissure getting wider and spreading out from beneath my right foot. Horrified, I leapt across the hole to other side but as I did so I heard a second crack. Without stopping to look I flung myself through the door and turned around as the entire cement floor disappeared into the hole. I stood on the edge of a thirty-foot drop looking down into a dark pit, and saw the stump of a tree at the bottom. Feeling a bit shaky I turned and walked back up the path to the edge of the compound. The panic soon subsided – I hadn't fallen to my death down the hole, but . . . I had destroyed the compound's only toilet and that made me feel awful. I was supposed to be helping these people, not destroying the little they had!

Jack met me where the path passed into the compound.

"Good morning!" he said cheerfully as he fell in beside me. "You didn't sleep too well, did you?"

I still wasn't used to the Kenyans' being aware of everything – they knew if I had a bad night even if I wasn't in the same sleeping room as them. I was only just beginning to realise that I couldn't even go to the toilet by myself, without one of the Kenyans watching over me. The guilt and embarrassment at what had happened increased.

"Um, Jack," I wasn't sure how to begin. "You know the toilet?"

He turned towards me looking concerned and stopped. I was forced to stop too otherwise I would have walked straight into him. Glancing back at the innocent looking toilet hut I could feel my face colouring.

The toilet in Obambo

"The floor just gave way!" I blurted out. It couldn't have broken because of my weight, surely?

I forced myself to look at Pastor Jack who was looking quite serious. He didn't say anything but carried on up the path to where the men of the compound had assembled under a tree. The Kenyans were all sitting down and listened to Pastor Jack intently as he spoke to them in their own language. Suddenly they all burst out laughing – real, belly laughter. I wanted the ground to open up and swallow me. The men were still laughing and talking loudly in their own language as Pastor Jack and I continued on our way back to our host's hut.

"Don't worry Monica," Pastor Jack said. "It'll all be sorted out. In the meantime, if you need the toilet, tell me and I'll walk you to the one at the next compound."

From what I had learnt so far, that meant the nearest toilet was a good fifteen minutes walk away at least. I determined not to need the toilet until the one I had wrecked had been repaired. After doing some preparation for further talks during my trip I noticed some of the compound men walking past carrying bags of cement. Intrigued I followed them down to the toilet hut. It was about 11am by now and sweltering hot. The men began mixing the cement with some bags of sand already there, combining the two with water. Suddenly Pastor Jack appeared at my side.

"Do you need the toilet?" he asked, glancing at the work going on.

"Oh no! No!" I said swiftly.

He looked at me and knew I did really, but didn't ask again. We stood there watching the cement being laid. I learnt later that it was not my weight that broke the cement floor at all. Real cement has sand and ballast mixed with it and it is the ballast that gives the cement its strength. I didn't know if the Kenyans could not afford to buy ballast or if it was just not available. What the Busia men in effect were laying was a screed that would have cracked and broken after some use anyway.

I spent the afternoon resting and preparing talks – however much I prepared beforehand, I never had enough material for a different talk in each place. I also handed over to Pastor Jack the £300 pounds cash that I had changed into Kenyan shillings to cover my expenses for this trip. I also told him about the £500 specifically given to Obambo by Battle Baptist. When I told him that altogether I had been able to transfer £4,000 for projects at Obambo into his bank account, he had tears in his eyes. Before sunset, Jack's brother Sylvester returned home. He had been painting scenery for film sets for an organisation in Nairobi.

Just before the evening meal was ready I visited the toilet again. This time the sun was not high enough to cause shadows and light to play across the hole in the middle of the floor. I shut the ill-fitting wooden door behind me and stared in horror as something writhed and twisted in the depths of the hole. Swallowing against the stench and my fear, I peered carefully into the hole. I stepped back against the door very quickly. The hole was full of white worms that moved ceaselessly in the muck. I spent as little time as possible in the toilet. I was determined not to be put off. I had been here in Kenya twice before, it was where I wanted to be so I was not going to be deterred by primitive toilet conditions.

NAIROBI TO NAKURU

During previous trips to Kenya I had travelled everywhere by bus. This meant that a fifty-seater bus would be carrying more than one hundred people plus their animals. Bus rides were not silent at all with people talking and singing and the animals making a lot of noise. Also, the buses tended not to have any windows that worked properly and some had broken glass which prevented the interior from over heating too much, but were also quite a health hazard! The first time I travelled in Kenya by bus I couldn't work out why my hair kept getting wet. I certainly didn't notice any unusual smell as the bus stank of body odour and animal droppings. It was only later in the journey that I thought to look up and saw a cardboard box full of chickens resting in the luggage rack above me. I had to wait until the following morning to wash my hair! Another time the driver of the bus fell asleep at the wheel and the side I was sitting on was taken out by a lorry driving in the opposite direction. It happened so quickly that there was no time to be scared and miraculously I walked away from the accident with only an one-centimeter scratch on my arm!

So when Pastor Jack announced he had arranged a car to take us to Obambo, I thought that it would probably be a great improvement on a bus ride. The car arrived shortly after breakfast, at 7.00 am driven by a Kenyan. The car was a Peugeot and had been registered in 1967. It was a type of saloon that would normally seat five people quite comfortably. I started bringing my luggage out of Sylvester's home and discovered a crowd of people around the car. To be honest, the car wasn't much to look at – it was a dirty, off-white colour with rust trimmings. Still, I thought, it must be better than going by bus.

The driver started packing my luggage in the boot – I had three cases as well as my hand luggage from the flight. He then proceeded to pack eleven other people's luggage. Pastor Jack appeared out of nowhere beside me.

"You slept well Monica?" he asked as if he already knew, nodding and waving at the people standing around.

"Yes thank you." I had slept remarkably well despite the continuous rain bouncing off the corrugated iron roof. "Who are all these people?"

"Oh, they are coming with us to Obambo," he replied cheerfully and started introducing me to them.

As I shook hands with them I wondered how on earth the car would hold us all. I didn't mind them coming along, I just couldn't see how we would all fit in.

" . . . And this is another of my brothers – Vincent, but I think you've met him before?" Pastor Jack was nearing the end of the line.

I had indeed met Jack and Sylvester's younger brother, but he was looking drawn and thin and his skin was dull. I wondered what was wrong with him.

"And of course Sylvester's eldest girl Fiona is travelling with us to visit her aunties in Obambo," Pastor Jack smiled.

The ten-year-old girl smiled back at us, showing her white teeth. Just then two men arrived carrying a mattress.

"Thank you!" Pastor Jack moved over to them. "Thank you very much indeed!"

He then proceeded to organise the other men to hoist the mattress onto the roof of the car. The driver produced something that looked like baler twine and with that they fastened it to the car roof.

"What is the mattress for?" I asked him as he came back to me.

"For you of course!" he said. "At your age you cannot be sleeping on the ground like us Kenyans. You need to take care of your bones!"

There was nothing really I could say to that!

Sylvester and his wife said goodbye to Fiona and I thanked them both for their hospitality. Then the twelve of us got into the car, which was a right hand drive. I sat in the front, next to the driver. Next to me was Fiona and on her left sat Pastor Jack. Somehow the other nine, including Vincent, who looked really ill, squeezed onto the back seat. After back-firing several times, the car roared to life and we bounced our way down the road.

The slum's roads were just dirt tracks with very deep pot-holes. Rainwater sparkled in the holes, but already in the heat of the day, the water was evaporating. Some of the potholes looked about a foot deep. There were hundreds of people walking up and down the track – children on their way to school, women carrying containers full of water on their heads, and other adults on their way to work. Sunlight gleamed off the corrugated tin shacks to either side, making the walls and roofs steam. Most of the shacks appeared to be one room with a small shop tacked on at the front.

With the windows wide open, the heat inside the car was already intense and I began to wonder if perhaps a bus journey might have been a bit more comfortable. With three of us on the front seat there was little legroom. I didn't really know what to do with my legs. I couldn't stretch them out so I bent them at an angle to the right. This meant that every time the driver changed gear he hit my knee. I couldn't really bend my knees to the left otherwise I would have squashed Fiona. I soon resigned myself to having a permanently bruised knee.

At length we reached the main road, the A104. The going was slightly better here as the surface had a covering of tarmac. Large potholes still gaped and threatened to trap the unwary driver. But it was early in the day and our driver seemed to be very alert. People were still walking at the edges of the road, their brightly coloured clothes standing out from the bleak, arid landscape. There was a real mixture of styles. Some wore traditional native Kenyan clothing. Others wore simple designs made from cheap material. And yet others wore, surprisingly, designer clothes. I enquired about this and learnt from Pastor Jack that they were second-hand designer clothes from the United States that the Kenyans sold at their local markets.

The heat increased as we travelled in a north-westerly direction towards Lake Victoria. I had seen some zebras in the distance out on the plains before the sun had risen too high, and there had been some baboons beside the road hoping we would throw food to them. I hadn't asked for the driver to stop so I could take photos, as I knew Pastor Jack wanted to reach Obambo before dark.

"It usually takes between eight and nine hours by car," he explained to me, as we were bounced up and down. "So we should be there by late afternoon."

That sounded good to me, though being stuck in the car for at least eight hours was not the most appealing prospect. I wondered, as my head nearly touched the roof, if the car still had any suspension left. We passed through Naivasha and Gilgil as the sun rose higher and increased in strength. The sky was a deep blue, a very warm, fierce colour. I wondered if I had put enough sunblock on and I felt I was being sunburnt through the open windows. The colour of the earth around us was orange-red, which was very different from the dark soil of Sussex. After a while however, the orange-red became oppressive and symbolised the intense heat that had even stopped the singing in the car. Great cracks ran through the strange coloured soil where the torrential rain of the night before had evaporated too quickly. I began to feel thirsty.

Our driver, although he continued to hit my knee every time he changed gear and bounced us around dreadfully on road, was in fact a very careful driver – by Kenyan standards anyway. We hadn't even come near a crash for the first hour and a half of the journey, when suddenly we hit something with a bump. The driver banged the brakes on with a squeal and we came to a shuddering halt. Everyone got out of the car and stretched their legs while the driver investigated the source of the bump. The heat was incredible and I could feel my nose burning. After a while Pastor Jack asked what was wrong. The driver took something metal out from underneath the car and shrugged.

"It's all right," Pastor Jack told us, "It's just the shock absorber – it's broken in two!"

I could feel my eyebrows rising in surprise. I wondered if we'd notice any difference. With a total disregard for my fellow passengers' belongings, the driver opened the boot and placed the shock absorber on top of the luggage. Then he got into the driver's seat and waited for us to climb in. The going was definitely worse when we set off again – even the driver noticed this time. He and Pastor Jack exchanged a few words as we passed Lake Nakuru National Park.

"We need to try and get the shock absorber fixed," Pastor Jack told us. "The driver knows a place that can help us – it shouldn't take long."

Buildings obscured the views of the wide valley and the far hills as we entered Nakuru. We turned off onto a dirt track and came to a halt outside one of the buildings.

"This is a place that makes agricultural machinery," Pastor Jack told me as we got out of the car.

The heat of the sun struck me like a physical blow. The air was so warm I could hardly breathe. Pastor Jack and the driver disappeared into the building and the rest of us milled around, stretching our legs and straightening our clothes. I felt so sticky and uncomfortable I would have liked nothing better than to have a cool wash. As I looked around however, I realised that this was the equivalent of a Kenyan industrial estate. The clang of metal on metal intermittently punctured the drone of the cars passing through the town. A couple of Kenyans accompanied Pastor Jack and the driver to the car and spent some time looking at the shock absorber. Nodding slowly they took the lump of metal away. And we waited. And waited. And waited.

As I waited I was reminded of an incident in the book of Ezra in the Old Testament (Ezra 8:21). The exiled people of Israel had assembled by the Ahava Canal and Ezra proclaimed a fast so that they could humble themselves before God and ask him for a safe journey. I thought to myself; had we even stopped to ask God to be with us?

My mind jumped to the end of Ezra chapter 8, to verse 31 where it says "The hand of God was on us, and he protected us from enemies and bandits along the way." I remembered the many times God had protected me whilst travelling in England. Then I recalled a previous trip to Kenya when I was travelling with Father Clement.

We were driving along the Eldorat road, well known for the bandits who lived in the woods. As we drove along we noticed bandits running out of the woods with guns on their shoulders, large knives in their hands and masks over their faces. There was a car some way in front of us which the bandits started to demolish.

"What shall we do?" I asked Father Clement who was driving.

"We'll tell the police," he replied, turning the car around.

About five miles before this point the police had been carrying out road checks but when we reached the place where we had been stopped before, the police had gone. An uneasy sensation niggled my stomach. I knew that often in Kenya the police and the bandits worked hand in glove. Perhaps the police had told the bandits that a white woman was on her way towards them. Father Clement took another route and I hanked God silently for keeping us safe.

In the heat of the day, waiting in Nakuru I thanked God again for his continued protection. I wished I could always remembered that Ezra made spiritual preparations for a journey before he made any other arrangements. The Israelites had known that God was in control and they couldn't make the journey without him. If I put God first in all that I did then I would be more prepared for whatever happened.

It was very difficult to find shade and I could feel my nose continuing to burn. I wanted to ask for the luggage to be unpacked so I could find my sunblock but that would mean more work for everyone. Several Kenyans came out and crawled under the car. One of them tried welding the shock absorber halves together and smell of solder and burning filled the air. It became apparent that there was a problem and several other workmen added their torches in order to secure the absorber in place.

We didn't talk much, it was too hot. If we did speak it was to mention how hungry and thirsty we were. I thought a lot about finding a toilet. One hour stretched into two hours. Then the fault was discovered. A spring was unsprung! Again the Kenyans from the agricultural shack disappeared, this time taking with them a rusty piece of metal, which was apparently the delinquent spring.

There had been people walking by all the time and now I turned my attention to them. Their brightly coloured clothes caught my eye time and time again. I wondered how they kept their clothes so clean with all the dust around and looked down at my crumpled, sweat stained dress with embarrassment. I glanced at my watch. Three hours had passed since we'd arrived in Nakuru. I wasn't feeling impatient, I had become used to African time. I was quite used to waiting and hanging around, but the heat was so fierce and I so desperately needed a drink and a toilet that I began to feel the heaviness of the hours.

The Kenyans returned from the building and attempted to fit the spring. There was a lot of talking going on amongst the workmen, so much so that I asked Pastor Jack what was going on.

"There is a spring," he replied. "And it will not stay put. It keeps coming off. Don't worry – they will fix it!"

I knew they would fix it but I also knew that it could take the rest of the day. I resumed my examination of the people passing by. In the distance I caught sight of some white people and deduced that they were probably visiting Nakuru National Park. The third hour passed and became four hours. And still the spring refused to stay put. The sun had passed its zenith and I was able to find a small bit of shade to rest in as the fifth hour of waiting drew to a close. Not that it was any cooler, but I didn't feel as though my nose was burning anymore.

At last the spring was fixed and the driver settled up the payment for the work. I looked anxiously at Pastor Jack, wondering if my expenses money would cover this extra item adequately. I knew that Pastor Jack would have to pay the driver back, in addition for the petrol and the hire of the car. I also knew better than to offer to pay it myself. As I was a white woman, I would have been charged an extortionate price.

It was mid-afternoon by the time we squeezed back into the car. Although it was a relief to be out of the glare of the sun, it was dreadfully stuffy and smelly inside the car. We bounced back onto a main road and I realised how desperately I would need a toilet by the end of the journey.

NAKURU TO SIAYA

The road between Nakuru and Kisumu stays mostly in the valleys but there are points where it ventures up into the sheer his of the Rift Valley. The hills rise up out of the ground without warning, towering up at intervals, dividing the vast valleys where the land is tilled and grazed. We were now driving in an easterly direction, heading towards Kisumu, still on the A104, when we were stopped by the police. In order to slow motorists down, the police put nine-inch high spikes in the ground. They then search the car for drugs and take a careful look at all the passengers in case someone is a criminal. The search was carried out swiftly and nothing was said about the overcrowding in the car – in Africa such things are commonplace.

Soon after we'd been stopped, we took a left hand turn onto a lesser road – the B1 – that was signposted to Kericho. We were in the hills now and every now and then the road swooped up into the rocky crags before plunging back down. There was one scary moment when the road veered abruptly up into the hills and for some time we were driving on a narrow track against the rocky hillside with a sheer drop to one side. Fortunately we met no oncoming traffic and quite soon the road descended to the valley again.

I breathed in relief once we had come back down to a horizontal part of the road, hoping that that was the worst part over. We travelled through a country of rocks and grass with a constant stream of humanity walking, always walking. Many of the Kenyans led donkeys carrying heavy loads. The driver suddenly braked at a corner in order to slow down slightly. I noticed his foot pumping up and down on the brake pedal as panic spread across his face. The car did not slow down, instead it sped up and careered off the road. One of the wheels struck a rock and everything seemed to happen in slow motion. The world outside the windscreen slowly revolved and came to rest with the sky at our feet and the earth near our heads. Something clanged loudly as if part of the car had fallen off.

No-one said a word and I was aware that I was sitting upside down, wedged between Fiona and the driver, with my mouth hanging open in surprise. I shut my mouth quickly, not

wanting to look silly. At the same time I felt absolutely terrified. Then I became aware of that quiet reassurance that I
knew to be God's presence and felt peace disperse the terror.
From outside the car came the sound of people's voices and
Kenyan faces appeared at the windows. With the windows
wide open, the driver and Pastor Jack were able to crawl out,
helped by the Kenyans who had suddenly appeared on every
side. I then followed the driver out, strong hands pulling me
through the window frame. My dress hampered me rather and
I tried not to look undignified, aware of the nine men still in
the back of the car.

I had no choice except to wear a dress as in the villages there
were very strict rules about clothing. Women wore skirts or
dresses; they never wore trousers. The cities were more cos-
mopolitan and trousers on women were acceptable there.
Dresses were certainly cooler to wear than trousers, but were
not very practical in an accident!

When we were all out of the car, the helpful Kenyans rolled
the vehicle onto its wheels. I thought that perhaps we might
have a rest to recover from the shock but it looked as though
we would be driving off straightaway. Jack's younger brother
was looking pretty shaky but his niece didn't look phased at
all. I looked around at the swathes of grass, rippling in the
gentle breeze. Back up on the road were more rocks and large
boulders. I suddenly realised how much worse it could have
been. A wave of panic engulfed me and then vanished. The car
could have ended up smashed against the boulders, or we
could have hit another motorist! I felt totally at peace though,
knowing deep in my heart that God had prevented us from
being hurt. Indeed, not one of us had a scratch.

Someone was walking to the car with a long piece of metal,
which they handed to the driver. He promptly placed the metal
on top of the luggage where the shock absorber had lain
earlier.

"What's that?" I asked Pastor Jack as he approached me.

"It's just the exhaust," he replied. "It fell off when the car turned over."

We had no brakes and no exhaust and I wondered what we would do now.

"Come on," Pastor Jack said. "We're going to push the car back onto the road."

The Kenyan men manhandled the vehicle onto the road by sheer brute force. After thanking those who had helped us, we got back in and drove off rather noisily. Before long we reached Kericho and left the hills behind us. The valley before us was vast and we chugged along erratically. Tea plantations spread out all around us as far as the eye could see. I managed to spot some zebras and a few monkeys as the sun sank ahead of us. I didn't enjoy that part of the journey. I was so tired and thirsty and really, really needed a toilet. We bounced up and down in the stifling heat, knowing we would not reach Obambo before dark now. I felt very tense as there were a lot of people walking at the sides of the road and was a bit worried that as we had no brakes, we might hit someone. At length the road we followed became slightly wider and Kisumu drew nearer.

On the outskirts of Kisumu we stopped and the driver tied on the exhaust with some more baler twine. He also fiddled with the brakes to try and make them work. By now it was getting dark. There was no twilight as in England. Instead, the sun disappeared rapidly and the clouds built up in the sky, bringing rain for the night. As we climbed back into the car we could hear the booming calls of frogs and the buzzing hum of thousands of insects.

As we drove off, past Kisumu, still heading west, I recalled the stealthiness of the night animals I'd seen on my previous trips. Once there had been a leopard watching me from the branch of a tree as I made my way to the toilet. I wouldn't have seen it but the rising moon shone straight into its eyes, making them gleam in the pitch dark. All the way back to the huts I had felt its eyes on my back. Another time there had been hyenas waiting when I emerged from the toilet hut. Their eyes shone with the reflected moonlight but they were on the ground and watched me pick my way back to the compound.

I tried not to think about toilets as we were jostled around and felt every bump in the road. I remembered that snakes came out to drink as the sun went down.

The first time I had seen a snake had been on a previous visit. A group of us were on our way to the market, the Kenyans surrounding me in a loose circle. I saw something move beneath a scrubby looking bush and was told by Pastor Jack to walk on a little. After a short while I turned and looking back I saw the Kenyans killing the snake with sticks. When they caught up with me they explained that it was a poisonous snake. Once we were having an evening meal in Pastor Jack's hut and a snake slithered in. Immediately the Kenyans set about killing it and I jumped up on one of the few chairs, imploring them not to hurt it. Pastor Jack explained to me afterwards that snakes are not allowed in the huts. If they get in and take refuge in the rafters it is very difficult to get rid of them.

The driver tried the brakes on a corner but whatever he had done to them didn't work. He had to wrestle with the steering wheel to keep us on the road. At least the noise wasn't quite as bad with the exhaust in place again. There was no-one walking the roads now and all the light had gone. Surely we must be near Siaya, I thought to myself, and remembered other animals I had been surprised by in Kenya.

One evening I had been in Pastor Jack's hut by myself and in the gloom had seen a creature rush along the bottom of a wall. It was large and moved swiftly so I thought it was a rat. Running outside in shock and fear, I called out to the people

in the compound that there was a rat in the hut. The Kenyans
nearby hurried inside and I could hear talking and then
someone laughed. Intrigued I walked towards the door of
the hut as my would-be rescuers came out. One of them was
carrying an extremely large frog.

"You think this would bite you?" they laughed as they let
the frog go.

Watching the frog hop away into the darkness I felt a bit
stupid. Now that I knew what it was, it looked nothing like
the rat I had assumed it to be. My friends then explained how
the frog had got into the hut. To get out of the heat of the
sun, frogs often go inside huts during the day. They like to
rest in the water tanks that are filled up by hand in the early
mornings and kept inside the huts to keep the water cool.
Once the sun goes down, the frogs make their way outside
again.

SIAYA TO OBAMBO

Siaya is the nearest town to Obambo and when we reached it
we stopped suddenly outside a shack.

"Just going to the hotel to buy some food," Pastor Jack said
as he opened the door.

The warm night air seemed like a fresh breeze after the
stifling smells in the car. As we waited for Pastor Jack I
noticed the driver dozing at the wheel and felt an apprehensive shiver run down my spine. To keep my mind off my fears
I looked around for the hotel but could see nothing except a
line of shacks on either side of the dirt road. In the gloom I
saw Pastor Jack coming out of a particularly dilapidated
shack carrying something in his arms. Before he got back into
the car he passed the loaves of bread to Fiona and I to hold.
The driver grunted and woke up as Pastor Jack slammed the

door and we started off again with a roar and a rattle of metal.

"Were these expensive?" I asked Pastor Jack over his niece's head.

Pastor Jack shrugged. "About 20 shillings for a loaf and 20 shillings for a pint of milk," he replied. (20 shillings equates to about 15p)

Cheap, I thought, but not to the Kenyans. I had drunk their milk before and knew I liked it. It was cow's milk. Although they kept goats, I had never known them to drink goat's milk in Obambo. As we jolted along in the humid night I remembered one particular goat on a previous trip.

"Monica!" called Pastor Jack as he came into the hut. "Would you like to take a photo of one of our goats?"

"Oh yes!" I said. I loved taking photos of animals and places as well as people in Kenya. The goats in Obambo had been bought with money raised by sponsors and churches in England, so I took every opportunity to make a photographic record of the community's success.

I found my camera and hurried out into the blazing sun after Pastor Jack. We walked along the path that eventually led to the toilet and found a group of men standing around a very pretty nanny goat.

"Why do you want a picture of her?" I asked as the men arranged themselves around her.

"We're going to kill her as we need the meat," Pastor Jack told me.

"Oh no!" I protested. "I'm not going to take a photo of an animal that's going to die!"

Pastor Jack looked quizzically at me. "She's old. She won't have any more kids, so . . . ."

I knew he was right. The community had very little meat and made the most of what they could get. But I couldn't bring myself to take her picture. I shook my head.

"I can't do it," I told them.

The Kenyans laughed at me as I walked away. Was I too finicky? I wondered. Am I still too western to fit in here? Later on that morning I left Pastor Jack's hut again once I had finished preparing my notes for the next few meetings and went down to the toilet. Just off the path was the carcase of the goat and the Kenyans were in the process of gutting it. My stomach turned at the sight of blood and internal organs. I decided, as I hurried on, that I wouldn't enquire as to what was in the supper dish that evening.

The headlights of the car illuminated a short way ahead of us, giving the driver just about enough time to drive around the potholes that seemed to grow larger with every mile that passed. We had now driven 300 miles from Nairobi and everyone was silent in the car, worn out by the heat and the journey. Suddenly the driver jerked the hand brake on and everyone plunged forwards. I stared out of the window, wondering why we had stopped. There was no gaping hole ahead, just a dark lump sprawled across the road. All the men got out of the car, leaving Fiona and me inside.

Although there had been no-one walking along the road, the bushes were suddenly swarming with Kenyans. Everyone seemed to be talking at once so I asked Fiona what was going on.

"It's a dead body," she replied, sounding very sleepy.

"Oh how awful!" I felt dreadful inside. "Is it a man or a woman?"

"A man," she said tiredly. "They don't think he's been dead very long. Uncle Jack's trying to find out which family he belongs to."

Despite the humidity, I felt a chill spread over my skin. No-one appeared too upset about the dead man, but I knew from what I'd seen before that death was part of life to them. Out here in Kenya life is cheap. People are always dying of AIDS, of violence, of malnutrition. . . . The dead man was carried away and Pastor Jack and the other men returned to the car.

We jolted on our way, the driver yawning continuously. I wondered how far he had had to drive in the morning before he came to pick us up at Sylvester's hut – that seemed like centuries ago. The driver must have been on the road for nearly fourteen hours now. The heat lulled me, making my eyes heavy and my head droop.

The jolting accelerated and I bounced awake as something crunched beneath the car and we came to an abrupt halt. The driver shook his head and sighed.

"Monica," I heard Pastor Jack say. "Can you help Fiona with the bread and milk. You climb out of the hole on the other side and wait for us."

In a daze I climbed out of the car and took the milk Pastor Jack passed to me. I followed Fiona out of the large pothole and looked back at the car. I really thought that the car had it. The two front doors were nearly hanging off their hinges and every time the men moved the vehicle the rattles and squeaks that came from the bodywork were alarming. By sheer man power the Kenyans hauled the car out of the twelve foot diameter pothole. By some miracle the car was still working and we all piled in again.

"Not long to go now," Pastor Jack said reassuringly as we lurched on our way again.

Obambo wasn't marked on the map of Kenya. The place where it was situated was marked as The Swamp on the north eastern shore of Lake Victoria. It was made up of ten communities and had 7,000 people living there.

On previous trips I had arrived in daylight and the first thing I could see as I came into Obambo was Pastor Jack's compound. The land ascended slightly on the approach to the village and there were many ridges in the road before the compound. I knew we were close when we started getting really jolted around in the car. Then the track appeared to level out and we stopped outside a hut.

As I got out of the car I breathed in the warm night air, dispelling the scent of body odour that had filled the car. I felt as though I was standing in an oven but that sensation was far more bearable than being in the close confines of the vehicle. On the air came that peculiar coffee scent from the bushes growing in the scrubland nearby and I knew I had arrived.

People were already appearing from the other huts in the compound. I turned to meet them, seeing the moonlight shining off the tin roof of Pastor Jack's hut. Away to the south I could see inky black clouds reaching up ragged fingers to cover the stars and smother the moon. Suddenly I was surrounded by Kenyans shaking my hand and asking how I was. Dressed immaculately in their mixture of traditional and home-made clothes, they were enthusiastic in their greetings. The only thing that I still found odd was that they didn't hug me – it was just not part of the culture in Obambo.

After we had all been welcomed, we started to unload the car and two men carried the mattress into Pastor Jack's hut. We had transferred about half the luggage to the hut when the moonlight vanished and it began to rain. It was as if buckets of water were being hurled out of the sky at us and we were somewhat bedraggled when we finally assembled in the hut for supper. Jack's wife Seline was boiling a kettle for tea and handed out the bread her husband had bought in Siaya. The rain pelting down on the tin roof made an appalling noise and was so loud that conversation was impossible.

As we waited for the kettle to boil I thought what a privilege it was to have a close relationship with Jesus, knowing that he would lead and guide me in every situation. Steam started to rise from the kettle's spout and I thought of water. Physical water was difficult to find in Obambo but the Christians around me knew that the Water of Life was even more important than drinking water. Their eagerness to know

Pastor Jack and his wife Seline

God more reminded me of Psalm 1:3: "He (that is whoever meditates on God's word day and night) is like a tree planted by streams of water, which yields its fruit in season and whose leaf does not wither. Whatever he does prospers." I didn't think that this meant that we would not face difficulties in our day-to-day lives (as the people of Obambo do to even find the water they need for daily living). What I thought it meant was that as a tree soaks up water and bears good fruit, so we also are to soak up God's Word, which produces in us actions and attitudes that will honour God. If I was going to do anything worthwhile I needed to have God's Word in my heart. If I was to say anything worthwhile to these people then my dependency had to be on God and His Word.

I drank the hot tea gratefully when it was ready and ate my portion of bread quickly. Some of the visitors were putting up a blanket in the main room of the hut to divide it in two. One side the women were sharing out blankets and preparing to sleep and on the other side, the men were lying down. After visiting the toilet in the pouring rain I made my way to one of Pastor Jack's storage rooms – room four was now known as Monica's room. I changed into my nightclothes, (this had caused much hilarity amongst the Kenyans when I first visited them, but they had now become used to my odd ways), and slipped under the mosquito net and blanket that had been laid over the mattress.

I was so tired but could not sleep straightaway. I remembered the first time I had visited Pastor Jack. There had been no extra rooms to his hut then and I had to sleep side-by-side with the Kenyan women. I didn't mind at all, but the rush mats that Seline had handed out took a lot of getting used to. Now Pastor Jack's hut boasted four extra rooms off the main hut. They were used for storing maize and millet and also the sewing machines that had been bought for the community. Visiting pastors would sleep among the food stores and the sewing machines if they had to stay the night.

The Kenyan ways had taken a bit of getting used to. If people were visiting Pastor Jack and the sun set, then the visitors would stay the night. So at a Friday night prayer meeting the whole house would be full of visitors sleeping side-by-side on the floor or on the rush mats. I twisted and turned on the mattress remembering how dusty and dirty it had got today. I was trying to remember what was stored in the third extra room attached to Pastor Jack's hut. Then I recalled – the third room was a bedroom for Jack, Seline and their children. The adopted children, orphans from families whose parents had died of AIDS, slept in the kitchen hut, which was separate from the main hut or in the animal hut where it was warm.

I turned over again, seeing the lump of my baggage in the darkness, framed by one of the tables I was sure I had seen in the main room of the hut on my last visit. Closing my eyes

I listened. The rain was easing off now and I could hear a squeaking noise, a bit like grasshoppers. In the distance there were dogs or hyenas barking and nearer at hand the frogs made a booming sound.

I was here in Obambo at last. Despite the journey and the accident, I was here where I was meant to be. Sleep came swiftly and deeply.

EASTER WEEKEND

Early in the morning I was startled out of deep slumber by the raucous calls of the compound's roosters. Further off I heard other roosters answering them and pulled the plastic sheets over my ears. I slept again, worn out by my journeying.

I woke again when I heard other people stirring in the hut and got myself dressed. Walking out into the heat of the early morning sun I felt a smile stretch across my face. I was really back in Obambo after so long. Standing at the edge of the compound I turned to the right and saw the almost western design of the house not far away that belonged to a government official. He was hardly ever there apparently, he just used it for holidays. Turning away I saw the mountains in the distance and the mud huts scattered across the red earth of the scrubland all around.

"Monica!" I heard Seline call me. "Your water is ready!"

I called my thanks and walked back through the compound. The sunshine gleamed off the tin roof making my eyes water. The other roofs in the compound were made of the traditional thatch. Pastor Jack's roof enabled him to collect and store rainwater and this was the advantage that outweighed the extra heat inside the hut during the day. The water collected from the roof was stored in a 6,000-litre tank which the Obambo Trust had provided for the compound. The use of this tank meant fewer visits to the muddy pool outside the village which was the only source of water for most people. Walking past the hut I could see the acre of land that Jack owned where they grew vegetables and grain in a good season.

The Kenyans had hung up some blankets on ropes in a square so that I could wash in private. The hot water steamed in a plastic bucket, which I regarded with trepidation. I had once stood in a plastic bowl of water in order to wash my feet and had split the bottom of the bowl. Another time I had sat down on a stool in order to wash my feet and the stool had broken underneath me. The worst time had been when I had had my wash and was carrying the bowl with the intention of throwing the dirty water away. Unfortunately I had slipped and fallen with most of the used water pouring over me.

This time I was careful, washing my hair before having a proper wash. I got rid of the water without any mishaps and returned to the hut for breakfast. The children were there before me and insisted on shaking my hand and reminding me of all their names. They were barefoot and some had orange coloured mud on their feet. I knew then that they were probably the ones who had made the journey to the water hole in the swamp in order to provide me with washing water. The adults bring back five gallons of water at a time in yellow buckets. The animals also use the water hole and the people of Obambo wash their clothes there as well.

After breakfast, Pastor Jack took me straight to the Convention he had arranged. The Convention was held in Obambo School and already a large crowd of Kenyans had gathered when Pastor Jack and I arrived. It wasn't far to walk from his hut to the school, but I was hot and sticky and my shoes were covered in red dust when we got there. The Convention had been arranged for pastors and Christian leaders in the area and I was the speaker.

We started off with very noisy and enthusiastic worship. It never ceased to amaze me how vibrant the Kenyans' worship was, perhaps because of their difficult circumstances. They had nothing and therefore were totally dependent on God for everything. After about an hour of worship in the increasing heat, I was asked to speak. We were out in the school grounds as the rooms in the school would not have been large enough to hold everyone there. I stood up at the front, with my interpreter at my side and began.

When I had first visited Kenya I had been totally unprepared for the amount of teaching I had to do. They expected a three hour session of teaching with only a break of between fifteen and thirty minutes before the next "seminar". To begin with, this regime had completely exhausted me and I had quickly used up all the notes I had prepared. But it was thus I became totally dependent on God to give me the energy to keep going as well as the inspiration to speak. When I looked back at the things I had said without prepared notes, I was amazed at how God had been speaking through me, speaking to the needs of my listeners at the time.

I liked being interpreted. I would speak about the first point I wanted to make and whilst my interpreter was translating that into Luo, I could look at my next point and get my thoughts together. So really I only had to speak for one and a half hours as my interpreter was very particular about translating my words. I took care though to make sure that I didn't finish before the three hours were up – I knew from previous experience that if I finished early, they would ask for more.

Most of the older generation of Obambo could not read and ninety-eight per cent of the Christians in the village did not own a Bible even if they could read, as Bibles were extremely expensive. None of the ministers in and around Obambo had any formal education or been to Bible College at all because those things just did not exist in the area. Neither did they have any commentaries or study books because they were unavailable and no-one had the money to buy them anyway. When I first went to Obambo I rather

*Everyone now has
a Bible*

naïvely thought that the Christians wouldn't know anything
at all but I was amazed at the way God had taught them just
through reading the few Bibles they had and through their
faith in him. Their depth of knowledge and love for God
were incredible and yet they were still hungry for more teaching. It was almost embarrassing to see their eagerness for my
talks.

On Easter Saturday I taught them from Philippians, from
notes I had prepared. This teaching was particularly pertinent
to the Obambo Christians at that time as they did not know
where their next job was coming from. I taught them that

Paul, the writer of Philippians, rejoiced even in his sufferings. Paul knew that God was with him all the time and that wherever Paul was, either in prison or a free man, God could use him through every circumstance to spread the gospel and bring glory to God's name.

We had a brief break for lunch and then started off with more exuberant worship, followed by another three hour stint of teaching from myself and the interpreter. I summarised my teaching on Philippians by reinforcing the fact that God works his purpose and plans out in all situations. I finished at about 4.00 pm when Pastor Jack announced we were then going to the marketplace where I was to do some more teaching. I didn't feel surprised, only a bit concerned because I had no more teaching notes with me! There was no time to return to Pastor Jack's hut and a large group of us walked a short distance to the market place.

The sun was still fierce but the Kenyans didn't appear affected by the heat at all. I kept wiping my face in order to appear as natural as they did but it didn't work. The market place consisted of a patch of bare red earth where the sellers sat or squatted by their wares spread out on blankets. There was a bit of food for sale as well as a lot of second-hand designer clothing going very cheaply. We gathered in a group and started singing loudly. The people in the marketplace looked over at us and carried on buying and selling.

Feeling very tired again I wondered what I was going to speak about to these Kenyans who were not Christians. Just then my attention was drawn to a group of half dressed children watching us. One of the boys wore a T-shirt with the words "You are valuable" written on it. At once I knew what I would speak on and joined in with the worship, thanking God silently in my heart.

When the worship stopped and I started to speak, a crowd formed immediately, masking the market from sight. I began with one of my favourite quotes from the Bible.

" 'Since you are precious and honoured in my sight, and because I love you . . . ' ", I said as the crowd started to form. "That's from a book in the bible called Isaiah and it's the writings of a prophet, a great man of God. In this section the prophet is recording what God says about his chosen people Israel but it is also applicable to us today. You are precious in God's eyes," I told them as the number of people grew and grew. "Even though you are sinful, God loves you . . . ".

The Kenyans listened intently to every word and I prayed that these words of mine, would be seeds that would one day lead them to Jesus. All the time the little boy in the T-shirt was watching and listening. Every time I was being interpreted I glanced over to see if he was still there. I concluded by telling them that it didn't matter what colour our skin was or what kind of background we had, God's love was constant and remained the same.

As I finished speaking, the market was packing up and people left in groups to travel home. We walked the short distance back to Pastor Jack's compound, talking quietly about things I'd said that day and about the people I had met. I was feeling very thirsty and tired again. When we reached the hut we talked long into the evening before eating the supper that Seline had prepared for us.

Sunday morning found me at the school again, with a large crowd of children. I had expected to teach them in the old church but apparently the building was too dangerous to be used. I taught the children for maybe an hour and a half before their parents and the rest of the adults turned up. We then had a vigorous time of worship into which the children entered wholeheartedly. Afterwards I spoke to the adults for about three hours, being interpreted as usual. The children sometimes stayed to listen, otherwise they played outside. Whether they were inside listening or outside playing, there were no disturbances, no disruptions.

Towards the end of our time together at the Obambo church, Pastor Jack announced that my church in England had sent £500 for the Obambo Christians for a new church building, which would be erected that week! This amount of money could not be spoken about in the village, however, as Pastor Jack would probably have been killed for it. The Obambo Christians understood about accountability, even though they found it strange. In a country where money will buy you food to stop your family from starving it was always tempting to use it to provide for short-term needs.

In the afternoon I met with the children again for two hours, teaching them the basic truths of the gospel. My two main aims were to tell them about Jesus and how his love could change their lives and to teach those who were already Christians how to pray. I taught them about what God expects of their lives as Christians and used the story of Joseph as an example. I explained that although Joseph's brothers meant Joseph to die because they hated him, God used their evil actions to result in a blessing for the whole of Joseph's family. In a way it was a similar message I had brought the adults the previous day – whatever was happening to these children, God was using it to result in a long-term blessing, even when the current circumstances were hard.

After the main afternoon session had ended, I spent some time with the children who were being sponsored by people in the UK. I had found sponsors for thirty-two orphans in Obambo who were all living with families from the church there. In Obambo the community had a responsibility for orphans. Other families nearby would take the orphans in and look after then.

Many of the sponsors had come from the south of England, where I was based, but there were others throughout the UK. Some people were sponsoring the children just for their education and uniform, others for their food, whilst others sponsored whole families. To sponsor a child who boarded at secondary school for instance cost £250 a year.

In Kenya there were between 100 and 120 children per class, which had recently risen to 400 per class, as fees for primary schools had been abolished. Whatever age the children were they started in the bottom class and stayed there until they passed the exams. There were eight classes at primary school and then, if the child's family could afford it, they went on to secondary school. The children had to provide their own books and pens and uniform. Most children were fourteen years old before they moved on to secondary school where there were only four classes to move through. Progress reports were provided every year for the sponsors and it had been seen that sponsored children were top of their class because they could now go to school regularly.

THE NEW OBAMBO CHURCH BUILDING

I had spent most of Monday morning and the first part of the afternoon preparing more notes for some teaching sessions the following week that I hadn't known I was doing. I had found that reading the Bible as much as I could in the little spare time I had was the best way to hear what God was telling me to teach on next. After ironing his best trousers, Pastor Jack had gone into Siaya to draw out the money sent by Battle Baptist in order to buy the materials for the new church building. About halfway through the afternoon I heard the sound of a car engine and put my notes away in my room. Pastor Jack had hired a car to bring him back to the compound along with his purchases, as well as the usual crowd of Kenyans needing a lift.

Jack's family helped him unload the car. I did offer to help but they shook their heads, saying I wasn't strong enough! He had bought some wood especially for the roof structure, a wheelbarrow for collecting scrub to weave into walls as well as tins and tins of nails. There were also some new hammers and several saws whose blades gleamed in the bright sunlight. At once the wheelbarrow became a plaything for the children as one of the older orphans wheeled two of the little ones around in it. They carried on like this for hours, not tiring of the game at all. They had no toys so anything that could be played with was a great treat for them. I remembered my first visit to Obambo.

I'd had a bit of a cold and my trusty paper hankies were getting used up. I wasn't sure where to put the used tissues so I asked Pastor Jack.

"Just put them on the floor," he told me. "Then the children can play with them."

I was horrified at such a suggestion. I couldn't let the children play with my used tissues – they could easily catch my cold! I was frightened that such an infection might kill them because their immune systems were so ineffective. In the end I secreted the tissues in my bag and determined to get rid of them somewhere hygienic.

The next day we started work on the church building. This one was to be nearer Pastor Jack's compound and the wheelbarrow was piled high with tins of nails and tools and taken down to the new site. It was just another patch of red earth surrounded by scrubland. The first thing to be done was to walk a mile or so in order to find several tall trees for the main frame of the building. Once the trees had been found, the men cut them down and the women carried the trunks on their heads to the site. I wanted to help and although I knew I couldn't carry things on my head, I felt strong enough to carry some of the branches back to be used for the walls. I had tried on previous visits to carry things on my head as the Kenyan

The church under construction

women did but everything had fallen off. I discovered that the children are taught from the age of about three years old to carry food and buckets on their heads so that by the age of seven they are able to fetch water without spilling it.

In the end I was only allowed to carry a few light pieces of wood back to the site because the Kenyans perceive white women as weak. In contrast to this, they consider black women to be very strong and allow them to carry most of the heavy things! As we walked back to the site I reflected on how things had changed since my first visit in 1995. Back then there had been a distinct division of labour. If the men were not working away from the village, they stood or sat beneath one of the few shady trees around their compound talking all day. If they wanted a wash or a drink they would shout for a woman to bring them water. From what I had seen then the women did all the work around the compound. The women and children fetched the water and looked after the little livestock they had. The women cooked all the food, did all the washing and cleaning and tilling of the land.

Pastor Jack ironing his trousers

By 1997 I had begun to notice some changes, but on this visit I was realising how different things had become. The men no longer sat around all day talking. If they weren't out working, they would look after the animals or till their acre of land. Although washing up and washing clothes were still done by the women, however I certainly wouldn't have caught Pastor Jack ironing his own trousers in 1995! I didn't remember actually giving them any teaching on this matter but it appeared that the whole community was now pulling its weight with the result that relationships between the sexes were less strained.

Whilst the men put up the wooden struts for the frame of the building, the women went out into the scrubland and cut the low, twisted bushes down. Being totally untalented in anything practical I wasn't much help but they didn't want me to do anything because I was the visitor. I watched the Kenyans working, amazed at their agility. They didn't have ladders, instead they cut tree branches to a certain length and fastened them together with string or nails to make tripods. They climbed up these tripods to secure the frame of the building with nails.

By that time it was getting dark so all work stopped for the day. On Wednesday they used the wood that Pastor Jack had bought in Siaya to make the frame to support the roof. They used the seemingly inexhaustible supply of tin sheets to make the roof itself and then the sides of the church went up – woven strips of wood and thin branches. Once these were secured I thought the building had been completed. But next came the long process of making a mud mixture from the red earth, animal dung and water and plastering it on to the walls, both inside and out.

When I was viewing the progress one day it came to me that the true church is not built of mud and wood, but on Jesus Christ (Ephesians 2:20) who is the chief cornerstone. I knew that nothing could overthrow the true church that was built on faith in Jesus and thought of Jesus' words to Peter in Matthew 16:10, "I will build my church and the gates of Hades will not overcome it."

In-between teaching sessions and further talk preparation, I watched the mud covering slowly grow around the church building. Every day there were about five Kenyans from the church working on the mud mixture, but the faces varied from day to day. I asked Pastor Jack about this.

"Most have no job to go to so they help with the church building," was his reply.

"What would they usually do?" I wanted to know.

Pastor Jack gestured to the scrubland around us. "They would work their acre of land in order to grow food for their family as most have no other income."

These people were such a challenge to me. My most frequent question whilst living in Obambo was "Why do good men suffer hardships?" I knew from my reading of the book of Job in the Old Testament that Job had a comfortable lifestyle and then suddenly he lost absolutely everything – his family, his friends, his home, his belongings, even his health. But Job continued to put his trust in God. He said, "I know that my redeemer lives . . . even though my skin has been destroyed, in my flesh I will see God." (Job 19:25–26). Job realised that there was a bigger picture, one that he could not understand. Job knew that his relationship with God, (eg the things that God was doing in him), was more important than the things that were happening to him. Job's relationship with God became stronger.

I felt God was saying to me, "Will you keep on believing in me even when things happen to you that you do not understand?" I learnt that being a Christian was all about my trust in a God who was alive. I had also learnt that everyone has a choice when things happen that no one understands, and the way is tough. We can either turn away from God or we can turn to Him and draw close to Him. We can either focus on our problems or we can focus on God. And the latter is what the people of Obambo do – they turn their eyes upon Jesus.

Just as it was getting light the next morning I saw a Kenyan from the church driving six oxen, one of which was blind, dragging a plough, breaking up the hard, red earth. The oxen had been bought with money I raised in England and allowed the Kenyans to cultivate more land and therefore grow more food. But the oxen couldn't guarantee the rains falling. And even if the rains did come, if they fell at the wrong time, the crops would still fail. Even though enough money had been raised to provide water storage tanks to collect rainwater from the church building that still wasn't enough if drought struck. I would talk to Pastor Jack about it – the next thing the village needed was a borehole for clean water.

Everyone who was available worked a long day on Saturday in order to finish the walls. Then on the Sunday after Easter Day we held our first gathering in the new Obambo church building. Early in the morning the boys and men walked up to the school and brought down the desks with the chairs attached to them and placed them in the new building, along with the six backless benches that had survived the dilapidation of the old church meeting place. The earth floor was compacted and very uneven and the backless benches wobbled a bit. Pastor Jack's wife brought down the rush mats usually used for sleeping on and spread them over the floor.

The new building started filling up and the worship that morning was especially exuberant and joyful. There were a lot of thankful prayers shouted out by the people that led into more loud songs. The people were lost in worship and thanksgiving and Pastor Jack prayed a long prayer thanking God for this new building, saying how wonderful it was to have somewhere to meet that was nearer the village. Other people gave simple testimonies as to what God had done in their lives during the past week. I was struck at how God-centred the testimonies were. It wasn't a case of "God did this for me, so I'm OK now," rather the stories were humbling and challenging, ultimately giving glory to God. Pastor Jack also announced that on Thursday I would be speaking at three communities north of Obambo and that if anyone would like to accompany me, they would be most welcome.

When the testimonies were over, I dedicated a child before I started to teach them. I spoke as usual for three hours with my interpreter patiently taking my words and translating them into Swahili and Luo. Several times during my talk a couple of the backless benches fell over due to the uneven ground and the number of people seated on them. No-one got more than a bit bruised but they still insisted on sitting on those benches. At the end of my talk Pastor Jack asked if anyone would like to be prayed for and a lot of people came forward. Together with the other leaders, Pastor Jack prayed for those who wanted it and they placed their hands on those who needed healing. It was a very intense time as the people cried out to God to change them and help them cope with their uncertain futures. As God started dealing with them their facial expressions changed and they looked as though they were in agony. The prayers were really heartfelt cries to God and most people were weeping. I just sat there, tears pouring down my face, actually feeling God moving amongst us in that meeting place.

LIFE IN OBAMBO

Everywhere I went in Obambo I met cheerful Kenyans, always smiling despite the hardships of daily living. They were hard-working but always appeared happy. With no electricity or running water, simple things such as washing clothes and washing up had to be done the hard way. Pastor Jack and his congregation focused on God and His goodness to them. They did not deny they had problems facing them every day but they looked to God to provide for them. Whenever I met people from the church they would be praising God for his goodness, singing spiritual songs and talking about the things God did. The few who had Bibles took them with them wherever they went and never lost an opportunity to study God's Word. Their favourite occupation was hearing the Bible expounded to them and all night prayer meetings were commonplace.

Even amongst the children I found this spirit of gratitude. If I handed out pencils and paper in my teaching sessions they were appreciative of such gifts and very willing to share the little they had with one another. The mortality rate amongst the children was still fairly high however. Pastor Jack asked me for extra money for some vitamins for a sick boy who was only three years old. I gave him the money immediately but tragically the boy died before the vitamins could have an effect.

Cooking lunch in Obambo

I was also asked to speak at the funeral of a five year old girl who had died of malaria. A few days before the girl had fallen ill but her mother had waited before seeking medical help as the journey to the nearest hospital was a long one and also, medical help was expensive. It wasn't until the girl's condition had worsened that her mother carried her to the hospital. On arrival the mother was informed that the money she had brought with her was not enough, she was 400 Kenyan shillings short. Leaving her daughter at the hospital, the woman walked back to Obambo to seek help. When she returned the hospital, it was too late for her daughter. The child had died because of a lack of medical help. She was the fifth child to die in that family – three died of malnutrition and two of malaria.

The Christians of Obambo are joyful in spite of their circumstances. Their eyes are firmly fixed on Jesus who they believe is with them in every circumstance. As I watched them go about their daily lives I saw their faith being acted out in their attitudes and reactions to whatever life threw at them. I was reminded of Paul's letter to the Philippians in the New

A five year old dies of Malaria because there is no medical help in Kenya

Testament where Paul could say "I count it all joy and rejoice in the Lord always" even though he himself was in prison. Paul instructed the Philippians that they should not focus on their outward circumstances but to be full of joy because whatever happens, Jesus Christ would always be with them. I thought how easy it would be for the Obambo Christians to become discouraged because of the unpleasant circumstances they often had to face. But I saw that they knew that their source of joy didn't come from what was happening to them, but from Jesus Christ living in them.

Our motto at Sunrise Ministries was taken from Jeremiah 29:11 " 'For I know the plans I have for you,' declares the

Lord, 'plans to prosper you and not to harm you, plans to give you hope and a future.'" I observed that these Christians really understood and believed that passage of Scripture. They knew that God knew their future. They knew that God's plans for them were good and full of hope. They had experienced time and time again God's presence accompanying them through the circumstances they faced – pain, suffering, hardship. And they were sure that God would bring all these things to a glorious conclusion.

One of the frequent psalms I heard on their lips was Psalm 23, in particular verses 5 and 6. "You prepare a table before me in the presence of my enemies. You anoint my head with oil; my cup overflows. Surely goodness and love will follow me all the days of my life, and I will dwell in the house of the Lord for ever."

THE THREE COMMUNITIES

On the Thursday following the first meeting held in the new church building, Pastor Jack reminded me that I was going to speak at three different communities in one day. These speaking opportunities were the ones I'd been preparing extra material for after Pastor Jack had told me about them when I'd arrived in Obambo.

"Where are we going?" I asked. "And how are we getting there?"

"Oh don't worry," replied Pastor Jack not answering my question. "I have hired a Nissan car."

With that I had to be content, imagining he'd hired some kind of people carrier. When the Nissan turned up it appeared as rusty as the Peugeot that had brought us to Obambo, but it was bigger and had roof bars. Already there was a crowd of people forming and I remembered Pastor Jack's announcement on Sunday. I counted the people waiting around the car – twenty five. Well, I thought, if a five-seater Peugeot can take twelve plus the driver, then the Nissan with twelve seats can take twenty-five. By the time we left our numbers had swelled to thirty two but we all managed somehow to fit in the car, even though there were mothers with tiny babies.

We headed out east, towards Siaya with the Kenyans singing loudly. Already it was stifling hot, the sun blazing mercilessly out of a clear, blue sky. Halfway to Siaya we came across a group of people waving at us. Pastor Jack told the driver to slow down and stop and then leaned out of the window to talk to them. They turned out to be more church members and my heart sank as I thought of more people squeezing in.

"I've told them I'll send some transport back to pick them up once we've reached Siaya," Pastor Jack told me as he sat down again.

We bounced along in the heat, the singing staying loud and happy. Just outside Siaya we found yet another group of people waiting for us. Again Pastor Jack spoke to them and then we drove on.

"I have to arrange transport for them too," he told me.

I think he was secretly delighted so many people wanted to travel so far in order to hear me speak. When we arrived at Siaya, the driver parked the car outside a line of shacks and Pastor Jack got out. I sat inside the car as it was slightly cooler than standing around outside. Most of the other passengers got out and stretched their legs and the mothers with young babies started feeding their children. Ten minutes went by, then fifteen. I thought Pastor Jack was hiring another car to collect the two groups of church members we'd passed. Time stretched out to half an hour before Pastor Jack returned.

"Everything's sorted out," he told us cheerfully. "I've sent bikes back to pick up the people. We'll just wait until they catch up with us here."

And so we waited as the sun rose higher in the sky and I felt thirsty. At length the people we were waiting for arrived – there were 3–4 people per bike! I noticed, as we drove off with the bikes following behind, that somehow the men had managed to get seats in the Nissan, along with the mothers and young babies, and that it was mainly women without small children who were riding the bikes. I wondered if perhaps I had been too hasty to conclude that all the rigid divisions had been erased.

Knowing my sense of direction wasn't that good, I wondered if I was at first imagining things. Having left Siaya we took a dirt track that gradually swung round so that we were heading west, with the sun behind us and slightly to our left. However, I didn't say anything, in case I was wrong and enjoyed the scenery as we jolted along. After about thirty minutes or so the driver stopped the car, said something to Pastor Jack and got out. I thought he had gone to relieve himself but as the minutes lengthened I asked Jack was what was happening.

"He got paid today," was the reply. "His house is just through the trees and he's gone to take his wife his earnings."

Half an hour had passed by the time our driver returned. The women on the bikes had caught up with us and were having a rest by the time we started off again. In the Nissan the Kenyans were still singing and I wondered where they got all their energy. We were heading towards Ukwale, which is north of Obambo and came to another town when Pastor Jack called for the driver to stop. Leaning out of the window he hailed a Kenyan on a bike and spoke with him briefly. The Kenyan turned his bike around and went racing off down a track to one side of the dirt road we were following. Everyone got out of the car to stretch their legs again. I got out as I was feeling pretty cramped from sitting too long.

"Why have we stopped now?" I asked Pastor Jack.

"I've sent a message to a woman who used to belong to my church," he said with a grin. "She moved up here a while ago and now goes to a different church. I've asked her if she'd like to come with us to hear you speak, so we must wait for her reply."

"Who was the man on the bike?"

He shrugged. "Don't know. Never seen him in my life before. But he's taking my message and bringing me back an answer."

Once again we waited and waited. Half an hour passed and the women on bikes caught up with us again and managed to have a rest before the man on his bike returned. It turned out that the woman Pastor Jack had known couldn't come with us so we got back in the Nissan and drove off again. This time I was sitting next to the door in the passenger seat and Pastor Jack sat next to the driver. The door rattled a lot, especially when we bounced over stones in the road. After a while we turned off onto a narrow dirt track with many potholes. Our progress was so slow that the women on bikes kept up with us easily.

I found it amazing that the Kenyans knew exactly where they were. There were no signposts and the area we were driving through was either a wilderness of scrubland, or forest. Entering one patch of forest the driver suddenly turned left and then right and then onto a very narrow walking path. The suspension in the Nissan wasn't much better than that of the Peugeot but so far the singing hadn't stopped. Pastor Jack started to talk about the three communities as we were jolted around.

"All three communities are served by three preachers from Obambo," he explained as the car swerved right, avoiding a large pothole. "But they only have one bicycle between them. So on a Saturday evening, before dark, all three of them travel on this one bike to Uboro. One preacher is dropped off there and the other two go on to Komenya Wangeluang where the second preacher stays. Then the third man travels on to Komenya Rabar. They all stay the night in each of their communities, preach on the Sunday morning and during the afternoon, the pastor with the bike travels back to Komenya Wangeluang, picks up the pastor there and then they go on to Uboro and finally return to Obambo."

Just then the driver slammed the brakes on and the car squealed to a halt. Ahead of us was a wide pothole that penetrated the scrub to either side. Pastor Jack and the driver discussed the situation.

"We can't drive round it," Pastor Jack told me as everyone got out. "So we are going to carry the car over the hole."

I stood in the sweltering heat in the group of mothers with babes in arms and watched the men manhandle the Nissan across the hole to the dirt track beyond it. Then we picked our way through the scrubland along with the women with their bikes and set off again. The door beside me was rattling even more now but I tried to ignore it as Pastor Jack told me which communities had church meeting places and which met in someone's house for church meetings. Without any warning the passenger door fell off with a dreadful clatter, making me jump. The driver applied the brakes and the red dust of the dirt track flew up and covered me from head to toe. The door was retrieved and fixed on again as best the driver could manage but I didn't dare touch it until we reached our first destination.

Uboro was located between Ukwale market and Siranga market and was really just an opening in the scrub with clusters of the usual thatched huts. As I got out of the car I felt a real mess. I had wiped the worst of the dust off my face with my ever-helpful paper tissues but trying to bang the dust out of my long dress just made things worse. I reminded myself that it wasn't my fault I looked a mess, but that I was here to speak and that God could use my words whatever state I was in.

As usual there was a crowd of people waiting to greet us. Pastor Jack apologised for being late, shrugging his shoulders and laughing about African time. No-one seemed bothered that we were two hours late and I saw Pastor Jack giving one of the men some money and sending him away to buy food. We were taken to the community's church building and everyone crowded in after us.

We started off as usual with a noisy time of worship and I soon forgot about my dusty dress. When I was asked to speak I stood up and taught them from the book of Zechariah in the Old Testament, focusing on chapter 4 and verse 6 " 'Not by might nor by power, but by my Spirit,' says the Lord Almighty." I was very aware that I was expected to bring something new to my hearers. I could not repeat any of the talks I had already given on this trip because Pastor Jack and those from Obambo would have already heard those other teaching sessions. And neither could I hope to repeat the teaching in all three villages today. Not only would I have the thirty or so people accompanying me travelling to the other communities, but more than likely the people from Uboro would follow me to the next two villages.

After three hours of talking and being interpreted, the air in the church building was stifling. I was really hungry and thirsty as well as needing a toilet. Once I had finished speaking and several people had prayed, we all left the church and walked through the village to someone's house. At this house a meal had been prepared, not just for those of us travelling, but for the entire village. The money Pastor Jack had given to someone earlier on had bought almost a feast. There was maize and millet porridge, lots of vegetables and even some meat.

As we sat on the ground, talking and eating, Pastor Jack interpreted what people were saying.

"They see all this as a feast," he explained. "Food is so scarce that anything like this is cause for a celebration."

I thought of the meagre £300 cash I had handed over to Pastor Jack when I had first arrived and was amazed that he still had enough left over to spare for food like this.

"Also," he continued, "We Christians see days like today as a double feast. We have a feast for the soul when you teach us, and afterwards we have a feast for the body!"

At an appropriate time I asked Pastor Jack if there was a toilet nearby and he went off to enquire. When he came back he told me the nearest toilet was at the church building! I felt a bit annoyed with myself as I realised I should have asked for the toilet before we'd left the building. As it was I had to hurry all the way back through the village with Pastor Jack trailing behind me, telling me we needed to be on our way again very soon.

The journey between Uboro and Komenya Wangeluang was shorter than I had expected. As I had thought, most of the Christians from Uboro followed us, along with the women on the bikes. I had only just gathered my thoughts and begun to go over my second talk of the day in my head when we arrived. The presence of a community was a little more defined in Komenya Wangeluang than in Uboro. The scrub had been cleared properly and there was evidence of attempts to farm the poor soil. The usual clusters of mud huts met the eye in every direction.

Again we were taken to the community's church building and started off with loud, exuberant worship. By the time I stood up to speak, everyone who was accompanying me had arrived. There were so many people in the building that when everyone sat down to listen, there was no room to move. I stood in a sea of Kenyans who watched me intently, listening to every translated word I spoke. I talked about Jabez's prayer from the Old Testament book of 1 Chronicles chapter 4 and verse 10 "Jabez cried out to the God of Israel, 'Oh, that you would bless me and enlarge my territory! Let your hand be with me, and keep me from harm so that I will be free from pain.' And God granted his request."

At one point during the talk, when I was being translated and glancing at my notes, I tried shifting my weight from foot to foot as I wasn't used to standing quite so still for so long. In doing so I stepped on a Kenyan's foot. He was quite a small man, a lot shorter than me. I drew my foot back as soon as I realised what I had done and apologised to him profusely. He smiled and shrugged his shoulders and seemed more interested in listening to the interpreter. I wondered just how much I had hurt him as he would have felt nearly the full force of my weight on his foot for a split second. I watched him leave the church building when I had finished and felt relieved that he appeared to be uninjured.

We left immediately for the third community as Pastor Jack commented that we were running a bit late. I thought this was a gross understatement as it was now mid to late afternoon and we should have been at Komenya Rabar several hours before. Again the trip was relatively short – for a Kenyan journey – and we soon arrived at our third destination. The Komenya Rabar community was well established with several acres of "farmland" around the village, but they had no church building. So we met in someone's house and people crowded outside, wanting to hear what I had to say.

After the time of worship, everything became almost deathly silent, so that those outside could hear the interpretation of my words. As I began to speak I recognised not only the people from Uboro but also a contingent from Komenya Wangeluang. I talked about the story of Joseph from Genesis in the Old Testament. I focused mainly on the differences in the ways Joseph and his father Jacob dealt with their situations. Despite the dreadful things that happened to Joseph such as being threatened with death by his brothers, sold into slavery, accused of adultery etc, he remained faithful and trusted God in every situation. This enabled God to bring him to Pharaoh's attention and thus eventually provide Joseph's family with a safe place to go during the time of famine. Jacob, on the other hand, dressed in sackcloth and ashes and mourned his favourite son's death. Jacob hung onto the past and at that point wasn't trusting God.

It wasn't until he was willing to give up everything he truly valued and let Benjamin go to Egypt that God brought everything together for him and restored Joseph to him.

When I had finished I was surprised to see food being served again. There was millet and maize porridge as before, as well as vegetables, but no meat. Everyone ate hungrily, discussing the talk. I was feeling ravenous and it seemed an age since the feast at Uboro. When the meal was over there were goodbyes to be said and those from Uboro and Komenya Wangeluang headed east, whilst the Nissan and bicycles headed southwest.

"We will pass through the village called Boro," Pastor Jack informed me.

Boro rang a bell – I had visited the village on my first trip to Kenya.

"And then we will drive to Siaya and finally to Obambo," he continued as the car jolted along the dirt track,

The Kenyans were still singing in the back of the car, which drowned out the sound of the fretful babies who had started crying. The heavy heat weighed on my eyelids and several times I felt my eyes closing. Pastor Jack chatted to the driver in Luo and sound of his voice combined with the red dust of the landscape to either side made me drowsy. I woke with a start to find the car had stopped at a T-junction. The road stretching away to east and west looked smoother then the track we were currently on and people walked up and down its length. Beside me, Pastor Jack was counting out some more money and handing it over to the driver. The babies in the back of the car were crying again and I yawned.

"What's happening?" I asked as the driver got out and disappeared.

"We've run out of petrol," was the explanation. "The driver's gone to buy some from Siaya – it's only about four kilometres away."

I thought that if a car ran out of petrol then the chances were that it wouldn't work again. *But*, I reminded myself, *this is*

Kenya and things that aren't supposed to work in England, somehow work over here. Everyone got out of the car and watched the sun descend rapidly to the horizon. It was a relief to walk around and stretch my legs a little. The babies had stopped crying and appeared to have fallen asleep. The women on bicycles passed us, waving and laughing. I was watching the last traces of the sunset in the darkening sky when I saw a cyclist pedalling from the west towards us. The bicycle wobbled a little as it approached, and then, as I watched, the machine just collapsed. The rider jumped clear and somewhat resignedly picked up the frame and started walking towards us.

"What is it?" asked Pastor Jack, suddenly appearing beside me.

"That person's bicycle's just collapsed, "I told him, pointing to the approaching figure.

The group of us waited around the car as the man drew nearer. Suddenly Pastor Jack called out to him and hurried to meet him. As Jack helped him with the bicycle I recognised the Kenyan. He had been the headmaster of Obambo School on my previous trip to Kenya but I could not remember his name though. Several men helped Pastor Jack and the headmaster secure the bicycle onto the Nissan's roof with the ever-helpful baler twine. The driver then arrived and put a gallon of petrol into the tank whilst everyone climbed back into the car.

The headmaster sat behind me and shook my hand firmly.

"Monica! It is good to see you!"

I learnt that he was now living in Siaya and teaching at the school in Boro. He missed Obambo School but the teaching systems are such in Kenya that the teachers are moved around every few years and have no say in the matter whatsoever. I remembered that he was a Christian and had played a significant part in the community at Obambo, but I still couldn't recall his name at all.

The Kenyan harmonies coming softly from the back of the car made me relax at last, even though the car still jolted over potholes. Only one headlight on the Nissan was working and it sent out a feeble beam into the close darkness. I felt sad knowing that tonight would be my last night in Obambo, and that tomorrow I must travel south to Nairobi and fly back to England the following day. I would have to get used to being around white people again, I thought, and then realised I was white!

Being the only white person in the car didn't make me feel out of place at all. These Kenyans were my brothers and sisters and I trusted them implicitly. I knew I was safe with them and that they would look after me if any danger threatened. I knew Kenya was not a safe place to be, but I trusted God to look after me and he had given me such wonderful friends in Obambo. I felt tears pricking at my eyes – I would miss the people terribly.

OBAMBO TO NAIROBI

My journey back to Nairobi started very early on Friday morning. Straight after a hurried breakfast I was packing my luggage into a "taxi". On top of my luggage were piled the bags of six other people. I looked at the small car and wondered exactly how many of us would be travelling in it.

"Don't worry," said Pastor Jack as he slammed the boot lid down hard and checked it was shut, "There's only seven of us plus the driver."

At least it was only to Siaya, I comforted myself. Pastor Jack's money didn't extend to a taxi all the way to Nairobi this time, so we were to catch a number of buses once we'd reached Siaya. When the final goodbyes had been said we set off. Pastor Jack and I sat in the front with the driver and our companions – five Kenyan men – squeezed into the back. The lively worship songs from the back kept my spirits from sinking too low as we left Obambo. I watched the red dirt go by as the sun rose ahead of us in a perfectly blue sky. I reminded myself that I wasn't actually leaving Kenya until tomorrow.

The journey back to Nairobi passed far quicker than the journey to Obambo two weeks before. We reached Siaya before the sun was too high and too hot and took a bus to Kisumu. We sat in a group, squeezed onto the hard seats and I learnt a bit about my fellow travellers. William, Jack's nephew, was quite a character. His mother was one of Jack's sisters who lived in Udida, which is close to Siaya. William was one of the few who had been able to go to Bible College and was now an evangelist on one of the satellite estates in Nairobi. His living expenses were paid by his uncle Sylvester. William was young and very enthusiastic about his calling as an evangelist, even though it was hard work.

My other travelling companions included Joseph, an elder in the church at Obambo and there were also two others from the church. People in Kenya travel together for protection.

We travelled southeast from Siaya to Kisumu where we boarded another bus. This bus was full of Kenyans who looked at me, surrounded by my friends from Obambo, with interest. The route the second bus took from Kisumu to Nakuru passed through the Rift Valley and I saw herds of zebra in the distance, as well as giraffes grazing on the clumps of trees to either side of the road. I got so excited about seeing them that everyone on the bus began to look out for animals for me.

When we reached Nakuru the heat was intense. We found the bus to take us to Nairobi, which turned out to be a small vehicle – just twelve seats. I wondered how many people would actually cram into such a small space. As our luggage was being loaded into the back of the bus, I noticed Pastor Jack asking the bus driver something. The driver nodded and then spoke to the other passengers waiting to board along with us.

"We need to get out before we reach Nairobi," Pastor Jack

explained to me as we climbed into the bus. "The driver is telling everyone else not to put their luggage with ours."

I glanced back at the pile of luggage in the back of the bus. I had three cases as well as my hand luggage and my six companions had brought along at least one bag each. We set off and at once the men I was travelling with started to sing loudly. The heat was soporific and I could feel my eyelids closing. Struggling to keep awake I noticed that there were only three other travellers apart from our group. Two men and a woman sat together near the front of the bus. They were Kenyans and the woman had succumbed to the stifling heat and was sleeping. She wore a beautiful blue scarf around her head. The two men nodded in time to the song my companions were singing but they did not join in.

The bus stopped on the outskirts of Nairobi and the driver threw our luggage down onto the bare earth. As the bus drove off in a cloud of dust we crossed the road and turned the corner to catch another bus to take us into the slums. We piled our luggage on board and squeezed onto the few spare seats left. The road we were following was wide and more or less smooth. To either side of the road numerous dirt tracks ran between rows of tin shacks. We had reached the slums. After a short while Pastor Jack asked the driver to stop and we went through the process of unloading our luggage yet again.

I was wondering how we would carry all our luggage to Sylvester's house and wondering how far away his shack was, when a young Kenyan lad ran up to us with a rusty wheelbarrow.

"Carry bags?" he asked me hopefully.

I looked at Pastor Jack who nodded and the heaviest luggage, (including my three suitcases), were piled into the wheelbarrow. We distributed the rest of the luggage amongst ourselves but I was only allowed to carry my hand-luggage. The heat had lessened slightly as the sun was angling down towards the west. The dust stuck to my dress and skin and I longed for water. The dirt tracks between the rows of tin shacks were numerous and I soon lost all sense of direction. The place reminded me of a warren and there were no names to the paths at all.

At last we reached Sylvester's house and could relax. Pastor Jack paid the wheelbarrow boy and our luggage was placed behind the curtain that divided the sleeping area from the living area. On my return from the communal toilet I found Pastor Jack organising people to go out and buy food. At length I was left alone with just Sylvester and his two youngest girls for company. Sylvester was pottering around, fixing the roof where a sheet of tin had come loose. The girls were playing quietly together and I was preparing some notes for the talks I might be asked to give that evening or the next day.

Sylvester had just brought a thin piece of metal into the hut and was trying to bend it into shape when I heard the empty rattling of a wheelbarrow. The sound faded away and I thought I must have been mistaken. Turning to my notes again I was surprised to hear Kenyan voices in the doorway. Thinking Pastor Jack and the others had returned early, I glanced up. Two men and a woman stood in the doorway and the tallest man, looking very stern, was speaking in Swahili to Sylvester. Jack's brother looked surprised and disappeared behind the curtain for a moment. I stared at the trio in the doorway thinking that they looked familiar. As Sylvester emerged with a black case in his hands I noticed that the woman was wearing a blue scarf. They had been our travelling companions from Nakuru to the outskirts of Nairobi.

Sylvester opened the case and I saw that it was full of papers. I couldn't recall seeing anything like that being packed into the back of the taxi that morning. The man spoke again in Swahili and Sylvester replied at length. Then, with a smile, the man took the case and the trio left.

"What was all that about?" I asked after Sylvester had watched them leave.

He shook his head and exhaled slowly. "That man, he is a lecturer," Sylvester replied. "He lectures at Nairobi University. He put his luggage in with yours by mistake and only realised his case was missing when they arrived in Nairobi."

"So how on earth did they find us?" I wanted to know.

"Because of you!" Sylvester smiled briefly. "They took a taxi to the place where you had got out and asked around to see if anyone knew where the white woman had gone. The taxi took them to the edge of the slum and the wheelbarrow boy was able to bring them here."

"Were they really angry?" I wanted to know.

Sylvester shrugged. "I think the man was worried about all his papers, but he said he wasn't too concerned because they had realised that Jack and the others were men of God. It was just finding the case in the slums. . . ."

When Pastor Jack and the others returned with food, Sylvester repeated the story to them.

"We're unintentional thieves!" I told them, laughing.

But the Kenyans took the situation very seriously. In no way did they want to be seen as thieves. However, the fact that the lecturer had recognised them as Christians, they found very encouraging. I could see that Pastor Jack had been upset by my flippant remark, so I cleared up my notes and waited patiently while dinner was prepared and didn't try to joke about the situation again.

TO NAIROBI AIRPORT

It was Saturday evening – nearly seven o'clock, and we were waiting in Sylvester's hut with my three large suitcases and my hand-luggage by the door. It was humid but the oppressive heat did nothing to stop the fervent prayers for my safety. Seven o'clock came and went and we left the hut, looking out for the car that Sylvester had arranged to take me to the airport.

"Monica can't wait too long," I heard Pastor Jack say to his brother. "She has to be at the airport by eight o'clock.

"I don't understand it," Sylvester frowned. "He told me he had no fares for this evening."

Shortly after that Sylvester disappeared for a while. He was driven back to the hut in a car belonging to another friend. My luggage was quickly stowed in the boot and as many Kenyans as possible crammed themselves into the back of the car. I felt sad and a little tense. I had to be at the airport for eight o'clock even though my flight wasn't until eleven that night. The car bounced over the hard earth to the main road. We made better time on wider main roads and had the airport in view when the police stopped us.

I thought of the airport and the time and knew that the police could hold us up for a good twenty minutes searching the car and asking questions. I didn't have time to form a prayer but I knew afterwards that God had heard the unvoiced plea in my heart.

"Where are you going?" was the first question.

"To the airport," I told the police.

They searched the boot in silence and I waited for the inevitable questions. I looked at the officer as he came around to the front of the car.

"OK," he said. "Drive on."

He waved us out as his fellow officer flagged down a car behind us. I breathed a sigh of relief, thanking God silently.

The airport drew nearer and I felt both glad and sorry. I didn't want to leave Kenya, I wanted to stay here with my brothers and sisters. I felt both tearful and at peace at the same time. God had been faithful and kept me safe from accidents on the roads, robbery and sickness. He had not deserted me but had given me the right words to speak in every situation. I had learnt not to let negative memories from previous trips adversely affect the present. Now I needed to return to England in order to raise more money for new projects at Obambo, but I still felt torn in two.

We reached the airport at five minutes to eight so there was not much time for goodbyes. I thanked Sylvester for his hospitality and thanked Pastor Jack for accompanying me on all my travels. I quickly thanked the Kenyans for coming to the airport with me and then struggled through the doors with my heavy suitcases. I looked back once to see them waving at me. Smiling I turned to find my way to the checking in desk.

As I waited for my luggage to be weighed and checked my flight times I felt annoyed that the Kenyans were not allowed in the airport. They had travelled all the way from Sylvester's hut to say goodbye to me as part of their hospitality culture. Now I was in the airport, I couldn't go back out. Once everything had been checked I still had nearly three hours to wait so I found myself a seat and started writing up my notes.

I wondered when I would be able to return and see the church I'd helped to build at Obambo. I wondered how many more would die before I returned and thought about Vincent, Jack's younger brother, who was too thin. The community at Obambo needed more animals and better farming equipment, as well as a borehole to get fresh water. The latter might stop so many children from dying. I wanted so much to stay in Kenya but knew I needed to go back to England and raise the awareness and the money to do what needed to be done.

When my flight was announced I slipped my notes into my hand-luggage and stood up. My dress was dreadfully creased so I brushed myself down and little clouds of red dust drifted out around me. I smiled and left my dress alone. The red dust of Obambo could accompany me home.

Vietnam Secrets

ALL BY MYSELF

God's protection in the midst of danger. God doesn't promise a world free from danger, but he does promise his help whenever we face danger. (Theme for Psalm 91)

It was April 2002 and I had just finished packing my cases for my first trip to Vietnam, when the shrill call of the telephone made me jump. I glanced at the clock as I walked to the telephone, realising I would only just get to the prayer meeting on time this evening if the caller didn't talk for long.

"Hi Monica?" said a male voice at the other end of the line. "It's Simon here."

Simon headed up an organisation called Global People, which was part of World Gospel, and he had invited me to Ho Chi Minh City in Vietnam, to train Sunday school teachers in the underground Christian church.

"Hello Simon!" I said warmly. "I've just finished packing! How are you?"

"Really stressed," was his reply, the emotion taken out of it by the long distance call. "I'm afraid I won't be able to meet up with you in Bangkok after all. I'm staying here in New Zealand for a while."

A cold lump of dread took up residence in my belly. "You're not coming on this trip then?" I asked, thinking I'd misheard him.

"No. I'm sorry it's such short notice too. But my contacts in Ho Chi Minh City know to meet you at the airport on Tuesday."

"Who am I meeting?" I asked, feeling very nervous.

"I can't tell you his name," Simon sounded really tired. "But you'll be met at the airport by a short, squat man. If he's late, call the number I sent you in my last email. Have you got your mask and hat?"

"I have," I made myself sound cheerful. "I've bought extra trousers and blouses too, so I blend in."

"That's good. Have a great time won't you?"

I stood in the silent house for a moment feeling dazed. I couldn't believe Simon had let me down like this. He knew I'd never been to Vietnam before, let alone visited an underground church. Thinking of all the latest reports from Vietnam, I felt chills spread over my skin. Recently, Christian meetings had been raided by the secret police so there would be heightened tension and higher risk for a western missionary visiting the country.

Giving myself a shake, I locked up and drove off to the prayer meeting that had been arranged by some friends. I was the last one there and the atmosphere was warm and welcoming. Relaxing a little, I let the singing flow over me and joined in the heartfelt prayers for my safety in Vietnam. I told the group that I would be going there by myself now and that I didn't know whom I was supposed to be meeting. My friends prayed at length about the situation and one of them read aloud Psalm 91. With each verse she read, I felt God's peace wash through me and the cold knot of dread in my belly disappeared. God felt it important enough to give me that Psalm for the trip and so I had the confidence that God would be with me in every circumstance.

"We'll pray through this psalm every day," my friend promised as I left.

The next day I was driven to the airport feeling amazingly at peace, despite the shock of Simon's phone call the previous night. The flight to Bangkok passed without incident and I found my flight to Ho Chi Minh City without any problems. I had eaten well and enjoyed the fish dish provided earlier on during the flight. Feeling really encouraged by the ease of the journey, I fell to considering the training materials I had prepared, wondering if I had enough for my meetings with the young people's leaders in the city. I had no idea where I was supposed to go – that had been Simon's department. But I felt calm and peaceful and trusted God to get me where He needed me to be.

HO CHI MINH AIRPORT

I will say of the Lord, "He is my refuge and my fortress, my God, in whom I trust." (Psalm 91:2)

Ho Chi Minh airport was small, with only a handful of planes leaving and arriving each day. I arrived there on a Tuesday just before midday, collected my luggage and wandered out with the other passengers to the area outside the airport. Opposite us was a roped off area behind which was a crowd of Vietnamese people touting for business. Feeling slightly dazed by the humidity and the noise, I gazed around looking for a short, squat man.

"Do you want a taxi?" some people were shouting.

"Which hotel do you need?" others cried.

The other passengers with me started to take taxis and meet contacts. I felt a sinking sensation in my stomach as I realised that all the men around me were short and squat and none of them seemed particularly interested in me. Standing there with my luggage on an airport trolley – a wooden, flat-bottomed affair – I tried to look like a tourist whose contact is just a bit late, but I was starting to feel conspicuous. As a westerner, the only safe way to visit Vietnam was to pose as a tourist. I knew I had to blend in and act like a tourist. I must do nothing to make myself stand out in any way. Soon, however, I was the only white person left standing outside the airport. Perhaps my particular short, squat man was late, I thought to myself, and tried to relax and not look worried.

Although many of those touting for business had picked up fares, there were still a reasonable number of taxi drivers left. They continued shouting at me for a while, until I announced:

"No thank you, I don't need a taxi. I'm waiting for my friend to collect me."

I noticed a female taxi driver staring at me with suspicion and decided to call the telephone number I had. Then I realised that I hadn't got any Vietnamese money and returned to the airport to change my sterling into dong (VND). There weren't any telephones in the airport and there wasn't really anyone around to ask after I'd changed my money. Wandering out of the airport again and avoiding the taxi drivers, I asked a passer-by where the nearest telephone was. The man told me to go to the Post Office and when I asked where that was, he just pointed to a shop several doors down from the airport. Intrigued, I walked along the pavement, wondering why there wasn't a big sign outside. To me the shop looked like an office that could have been part of the airport!

The man opened the door for me and followed me inside. The shop was small and bare of furniture except for a counter to the left with a telephone on it. Behind the counter sat a middle-aged woman who smiled as I walked in.

"Use the phone," the man told me as I dragged my trolley full of luggage over to the counter.

"How much does it cost?" I asked, finding my notebook in my hand luggage.

Both the Vietnamese shrugged, indicating that I paid for the call when I finished. Finding the number in my notebook, I picked up the telephone and pressed the buttons. Nervously I waited whilst the telephone rang at the other end, aware of he man and woman watching me. A woman's voice answered the telephone and a rush of adrenalin made my mind go blank.

"Ah, hello!" I managed to say, trying to look relaxed. "It's Monica Cook here."

"Hello Monica!" the woman sounded surprised.

"I'm here at the airport."

"Oh we expect you not until this evening," came the reply in broken English.

"Can you pick me up now?" I asked slowly.

"We pick up at 6.00 pm," was the answer.

Fighting to keep worry from my face in case I made the man and woman with me suspicious, I smiled at the phone.

"But I'm here now and I'm not sure where I'm supposed to go."

"OK," came the hesitant reply. "We pick up you now."

The line went dead and I replaced the receiver. "How much do I owe you?" I asked the woman at the counter.

To my surprise the cost was minimal and I left the Post Office, thanking the man who had taken me there. Pulling my luggage along, I returned to the airport and waited, trying to ignore the people touting for business. The woman I had noticed earlier pushed her way to the front of the crowd.

"Where you go?" she demanded. "I take you there now!"

"I take you!" cried a man with a loud voice.

"It's OK," I said, smiling, "My friend is coming to pick me up now."

The minutes ticked by, five minutes stretching to ten then fifteen and twenty.

"Who is your friend?" the female taxi driver wanted to know, "Where is your friend coming from?"

I ignored her, staring up and down the road. Nearly half an hour had passed.

"You tell me now who your friend is!" the woman shouted, her dark eyes gleaming menacingly at me.

QUANG HOTEL

He who dwells in the shelter of the Most High will rest in the shadow of the Almighty. (Psalm 91:1)

An oversized moped came chugging along the street with two people riding it. The driver was short and squat and the woman behind him was slim. The moped slowed to a halt before me and the woman jumped off.

"Monica Cook?" she enquired, looking up at me. "I'm Leah. We've come to take you to your hotel."

I sighed with relief and greeted my contacts. Then I looked at the moped and back at my large case, holdall and hand luggage. We'd never get my luggage on the moped! My contacts conferred with each other whilst the taxi drivers fell silent and looked around for more fares. The menacing woman had withdrawn to the back of the crowd. Just then the man turned the moped around and drove away.

"We get taxi," Leah explained and turned to the waiting taxi drivers.

To my relief it was the man with the loud voice who was chosen by Leah to convey us to my hotel. I noticed the menacing woman still staring at me from the back of the crowd. The taxi driver brought his car to where we were waiting and piled my luggage into the boot. Leah and I sat in the back and attempted to talk. Leah's English was very limited and once we were in traffic, I found it hard to concentrate on anything at all.

Our taxi was a smallish, black car that wove in and out of the traffic, which consisted mainly of motorcycles, but there were a number of other taxis to be seen as well. My first impression was that there was no traffic control whatsoever.

Cars and motorcycles drove at all angles and in all directions. If our taxi driver saw a hole in the traffic he drove into it and stopped, waiting for the next gap to appear. Sometimes someone else got to the gap before we did, so the taxi driver just slammed the brakes on and stopped. There was no swearing and cursing and there even appeared to be a kind of respect for the other drivers. Somehow we managed to avoid accidents. And although our progress was erratic and our way appeared to be passing through an endless traffic jam, the traffic constantly moved. The driving was certainly aggressive and I felt as though my heart had taken up residence in my mouth.

On reaching Hotel Quang I found my purse in order to pay the taxi driver. I really thought I had worked out the correct amount but the taxi driver actually took more money from my hand! Leah unloaded my luggage and the taxi drove off. I looked around and discovered I was in a narrow street with tall buildings on either side. The entire street appeared to be hotels and restaurants. Signs hung from walls, jutting out into the street with the names of the hotels on them such as Linh and Nu Lan. On both sides of the road there were motorbikes parked and there appeared to be no pavement, just a concrete road.

Leah helped me carry my luggage to the hotel and I checked in. Hotel Quang was quite prestigious, being the first hotel ever to open in Vietnam. I was expecting something quite western but everything appeared very basic. I had to stay in a hotel as westerners were not allowed to stay with the Vietnamese people. My room was practically bare which I found a bit of a shock but Leah placed my luggage on the floor, and once the proprietor had left us alone, said;

"Be ready at 8.00 am tomorrow. Someone on a motorbike will collect you."

And with that she had gone. Who? I wanted to ask. And where will I be going? But I knew that Leah could not tell me.

She probably didn't know all the details herself, that way the underground church avoided detection.

I looked around my room. There were two single beds opposite the door, each with a hard mattress. There were no covers on the beds due to the humidity – already I was perspiring. Each bed had a sheet over the mattress and a pillow. The walls were whitewashed and the floor was covered in lino. There were no drawers only a closet in the corner opposite the en suite facilities. Above the beds was a small, square window looking out onto a tiled roof. I was reminded of a prison cell and laughed at myself. My en suite facilities consisted of a toilet and a cold shower in the corner along from the beds. Taking a quick glance outside my room, I saw other doors and a long, wide corridor. I was not far from the stairwell, which reminded me of flats in England.

Returning to my room I started unpacking. I hung my dresses up in the closet and used my case as a drawer on the spare bed. I started sorting out my training materials when I suddenly felt ill.

FOOD POISONING

You will not fear the terror of night, nor the arrow that flies by day, nor the pestilence that stalks in the darkness, nor the plague that destroys at midday." (Psalm 91:5–6)

Staring at my notes, I realised I couldn't make head or tail of the typing. Feeling nauseous I put the notes back and lay down on my bed, hoping the feeling would pass. It didn't. It got worse. I think it must have been about 4.00 pm by now and I lay there feeling dreadful. I had been thinking about wandering along the street to find somewhere to eat supper but now the thought of food made me feel awful. I remembered reading somewhere about the temperature being around thirty-eight degrees and the humidity being eighty-five per cent. Everything I was wearing was soaked and the sheet felt drenched beneath me. I hardly had enough energy to lift my head from the pillow when the proprietor knocked on my door asking for my passport.

"I'll get it in a minute," I remember saying faintly.

Somewhere in my delirium I recalled that Vietnamese law required hotel proprietors to hold the passports of their customers. I couldn't bring to mind the reason why but I knew I didn't have enough strength to get off the bed and find it. My mind fell to thinking about the next day. How on earth was I going to ride a motorbike in this condition? I wasn't sure I'd even be able to navigate the stairs. Waves of nausea engulfed me and several times the proprietor's wife knocked on my door, requesting my passport.

At last I crawled off the bed and managed to find my passport and give it to the proprietor's wife. Then I collapsed on the bed again. Still feeling sick and ill, my mind explored the easons why I was ill. It couldn't be the heat, I'd been in hot countries before. Perhaps the humidity was affecting me. And then I remembered. A little picture floated into my mind of that lovely fish dish I'd eaten during the flight. Fish. Food poisoning. I groaned, banishing the picture from my mind.

The illness lasted between nine and ten hours and in the early morning I fell asleep. My sleep was shallow and brief but by six am I felt so much better, just incredibly weak. How on earth was I going to make it through the day? I was shaky inside when I took a cold shower but felt refreshed afterwards.

"Lord, you'll have to help me through today," I prayed as I got dressed. "I feel dreadful and I've got a whole day of training to do."

I changed into a pair of my new black trousers and chose one of new coloured tops. My hands were still shaky as I went through my training materials and without really knowing what I was doing, I bundled some things into my holdall. Memory verses tumbled into the bag along with quizzes, stories and the three ropes that become one rope. I couldn't even recall what I was supposed to be teaching on today so I crammed some Bible stories into the bag, as well as activity games.

Feeling really thirsty, I wandered out of the hotel at about seven am and walked along the road looking at the restaurants. The smell of cooking food made me feel a bit queasy still and I came back to a little place on the same side as Hotel Quang. There was an Internet café situated upstairs which I thought might be useful when I was feeling better again. I ordered water and bread and sat down. I watched other customers order fresh fruit juice which looked rather appetising. I could just about stomach the bread and water when it arrived and decided to leave the fruit juice for another day.

I suddenly realised that it was nearly eight am and that my holdall was still in my room in the hotel. Hurrying back to Hotel Quang I picked up my holdall, cap and scarf and was downstairs again on the dot of eight o'clock.

HO CHI MINH CITY

If you make the Most High your dwelling – even the Lord, who is my refuge – then no harm will befall you, no disaster will come near your tent. (Psalm 91:9–10)

"This is my first time here," I was telling the proprietor. "I don't really know anyone at all! I'm looking forward to seeing the City," I added, recalling I was supposed to be a tourist.

Just then a motorbike drew up outside with a small, slight woman driving it.

"Oh this must be my lift for today!" I said and hurried outside. It suddenly struck me that I'd just contradicted myself. Glancing back at the proprietor I saw that he was busy. Perhaps he hadn't understood all I had said to him.

"Monica Cook?" asked the lady riding the motorbike. "I'm Judith, I'm one of the organisers of CMS. Have you ever ridden a motorbike before?"

"Hello Judith!" I said warmly, despite feeling really weak and shaky still. "No, I've never ridden a bike before!"

"OK," said Judith, "Just hold on to me and do what I do. When we arrive at the church, you must walk to the door normally – not too quickly but not too slowly. You mustn't be noticed."

I climbed aboard feeling nervous and put my cap on. After tying my scarf over my face I arranged my canvas holdall on my lap, cradling it with one arm. With my other hand I held onto Judith's waist. I felt really stupid. I was trying to blend in and look like a tourist, but here I was dressing up like a Vietnamese! Simon's idea had been that I would blend in by wearing dark trousers and coloured tops and in order to travel by motorbike you had to wear a hat and mask. The mask or scarf was to prevent you from inhaling the fumes. I noticed that Judith was wearing gloves as well and learnt later that the Vietnamese cover up in order not to get suntanned. I sighed. I was twice the height of most Vietnamese so I didn't really look like them at all. Neither did I look like a tourist. No amount of clothing could hide the fact that I was tall and took a size twenty in most clothes.

Judith started the motorbike and we drove off. I clutched at her blouse and swayed dangerously. Driving down the hotel road wasn't too bad but soon we turned a corner and drove out into a sea of traffic. The noise was horrendous, engines roared and purred. Again there appeared to be no rule of the

Monica in disguise

road but at least this morning all the traffic was going in one direction. After two minutes my cap flew off.

"Judith stop!" I yelled in her ear. "My hat's come off."

She didn't even acknowledge she'd heard me. Judith just swung the motorbike around with me clutching desperately at her waist and we were now driving against the flow of traffic. I was terrified. We wove in and out of the oncoming bikes just avoiding collisions time and time again. Then Judith stopped abruptly, bent down and picked my hat up. I quickly jammed the cap on my head before she swung the motorbike around again.

The constant noise of engines became wearing and I wondered again how I was going to get through the day. There were people shouting over the noise of the engines and the heat was intense. Everyone seemed to be trying to get somewhere quickly and on the street corners I saw children begging. Around me was a sea of covered faces and conical hats.

All at once we started weaving in and out of the traffic, travelling across the street and at length I saw why. We were heading for a side street and at last reached the relative peace of a quiet road. The motorbike slowed down and halted.

"Go now," Judith said quietly. "Walk normally – it's that building ahead on the left. Don't look back at me."

I dismounted from the motorbike and walked casually towards the church building.

THE CMS CHURCH

"Because he loves me," says the Lord, "I will rescue him;
I will protect him, for he acknowledges my name."
(Psalm 91:14)

True Christianity is forbidden in Vietnam. The government is Communist and eighty per cent of the population are Buddhists. Buddhism is permitted and there are temples everywhere, their golden spires rising up and catching the sunlight. The only Christian church that is recognised, is the CMS church. (I never did discover what the letters stood for). But the Christians belonging to the CMS church are forbidden to have any contact with Westerners and they are also forbidden to speak about the Holy Spirit.

I noticed people standing around outside the church building as well as people hanging around at the entrance to the church as I approached. Their eyes slid over me, focusing on those passing by and I felt a shiver of apprehension pass down my spine. I entered the building and found it quite ornate and spacious. A Vietnamese man on the stairs that led out of the foyer, beckoned to me and I followed him up to the first floor. Without saying a word the man opened a door and closed it again behind me.

Feeling suffocated by my scarf, I quickly unwound it from across my face and placed it in my bag, along with my cap. Looking around, my eyes were drawn to the banner at the far end of the room. It was large and square and nearly covered the end wall. The cloth was black ith a thin red cross at the centre and silver rays of light issued from behind the cross. The design was so simple but very effective. I was aware of a group of people waiting for me and one of the ladies came forward to greet me.

"Monica! I am Esther. I'm the rep for the Scripture Union in Ho Chi Minh City. How are you?"

I smiled back at her, feeling really shaky.

"OK," I replied, not wanting to let on that I felt absolutely dreadful.

"Before we begin," said Esther leading me towards the banner, "You must be aware that the secret police could raid us at any time."

My stomach clenched with cold fear which dissipated immediately. I knew God was watching over me, that's what Psalm 91 had promised.

"If we are raided," Esther continued, "You must not be found with us. You must leave immediately through this trap door."

She pushed the banner aside and when she opened a trap door in the floor, I could see a spiral staircase leading down into darkness.

"This will take you to the back of the church and when you reach the ground you must just walk normally until you are a long way from the building. Then you can find a taxi to take you back to your hotel."

"How will we know if there is a raid?" I asked.

"Someone on the stairs will signal to us," Esther told me. "You won't see or hear the signal, one of us will just tell you to go through the trap door."

I wondered then if the people in the foyer were watchers for the secret police.

"How can you tell who the secret police are?" I wanted to know as Esther closed the trap door and twitched the banner back into place.

"You can't tell, they're in plain clothes," she said as she led me back to the group of young men and women waiting for me.

We settled ourselves in that large, airy, upstairs room and the meeting began. During the prayer time at the beginning, my thoughts whirled so fast they nearly tripped over themselves. I stared at the people around me. These Christians faced imprisonment and torture if they were caught here with me. But they were willing to come together and be trained and the risk of torture didn't put them off. I knew that I would be banned from ever entering Vietnam again if I was caught with these Christians, and things would have looked quite bad for Global People too.

The Christians soaked up my training just as bone-dry sponges soak up water. There hadn't been any Sunday schools or anything similar for twenty-five years due to the war. With a communist government in power and the church being underground, two generations of people had grown up in Vietnam without any Christian teaching. As Christianity grew slowly in the country, the Christians had to teach themselves. I learnt that this small group I was teaching were only a handful of the hundreds of unofficial Sunday school teachers who had never had any children's training at all. This is where Global People came in. Global People would organise someone to come in and train some of the Christians. Those Christians would then teach others.

All that day I felt very weak as a result of the food poisoning the previous day. I felt quite poorly really but a verse kept popping into my head every time I wanted to give up – "When we are weak, God is strong." That promise proved true that day! I trained from 9.00 am until 5.00 pm but we did have quite a long break for lunch which was a relief. We stopped at

11.30 am for lunch – not that I really felt like eating much – and when we had eaten, we all lay down on the floor and went to sleep until about 1.15 pm when people started waking up again. I needed that sleep! Apparently everything stops in Vietnam during the hottest part of the day. At 5.00 pm, when we finished I was taken back to my hotel by Judith on her motorbike. On the way back I wondered how many of the people we passed were actually secret police.

STREET CHILDREN

He will cover you with his feathers, and under his wings you will find refuge. (Psalm 91:4a)

The humidity was high that evening so I had a cold shower when I returned to Hotel Quang and then decided to try and eat supper. Although I was exhausted it felt nice to be able to think – where shall I eat tonight? As I walked along, I was aware of people staring at me but I didn't feel as though the secret police were going to pounce on me. I wandered along the street until I reached the restaurant I'd had breakfast at. The food was relatively cheap and I was feeling quite hungry by now. After my meal I visited the Internet café upstairs and emailed my colleague Barry, to let him know I'd arrived safely and had completed my first day of training. As my eyes felt heavy I wandered back to the hotel and went to bed as I knew I would have to be ready at 8.00 am again the next morning for my lift to the CMS church.

I discovered that there was always someone on duty at Hotel Quang. They would see me coming up the road and get my room key ready for me when I arrived. We would always have a chat, particularly in the mornings if my lift was late.

Spiritually, the Vietnamese had nothing. Therefore the spread of Christianity was growing and the teaching amongst Christians kept on spreading. Not only did the Vietnamese Christians risk their lives by becoming Christians, they also risked their lives in trying to help others. I discovered that the children I'd seen begging on the street corners were just a few of the thousands of street children in Ho Chi Minh City. No-one cared about them and their only source of food was from the dustbins at the backs of the hotels. Initially Global People tried feeding the children but the communist government forbade it.

The feeding of the street children still continued however. A few people from different churches decide to feed the children and they pray-in the money to buy the rice. They choose an area and have two teams standing by with the whole operation overseen by Global People. The first team takes a barrow load of food to feed 150 street children, feeds them quickly but they don't speak to them. This team is then moved on by the police and once the police have disappeared, team two takes to the streets and talks to the children who have just been fed. They talk about Jesus and becoming a Christian. The police can never link the two groups and many of the children have come to know Jesus because they had first been fed.

The Christians risk their lives doing this kind of thing as the government are opposed to any form of evangelism. But the Christians from different churches are united in their desire to help these destitute children. The other vision these Christians have is to open an orphanage, as that is permitted by the government. Their aim would be to not only feed and clothe the children, but to tell them about Jesus too.

There are no Christian bookshops at all in Vietnam so the Christians have to rely on resources from abroad. As you can't send literature in bulk, western Christians smuggle books in secretly or they are sent in the post one at a time. I had specifically brought extra training materials with me in order to leave most of them behind. I tried to use simple, everyday materials that wouldn't cost a lot of money to buy such as newspapers, paper and scissors. I couldn't use PowerPoint in Vietnam but I could use pebbles!

TOURIST

A thousand may fall at your side, ten thousand at your right hand, but it will not come near you. You will only observe with your eyes and see the punishment of the wicked. (Psalm 91:7–8)

Training on Thursday and Friday went very well and I felt back to normal again. My technique of playing games as part of my training went down very well with the Vietnamese! On Thursday evening I met up with David, the co-ordinator for Global People in Ho Chi Minh City and we ate supper at my, now, favourite restaurant.

On Friday evening I had a surprise visit from Simon himself and took him out to the restaurant for supper. He felt he had to come to Vietnam as he didn't feel it was right, leaving me by myself for all that time. He apologised in a vague sort of way and went straight into plans over supper. It turned out he was only staying the weekend and was booked in at Hotel Quang. On Monday he would be flying off somewhere else to meet his wife. His New Zealand accent sounded bizarre in the restaurant that was full of Vietnamese people.

"I'll do training at CMS tomorrow," he told me, "You have the day off – go and do some tourist things!"

"Where's the best place to go?" I asked.

"Try the War Museum," Simon suggested.

That didn't sound particularly pleasant, but I made a note of it.

"On Sunday we'll be going to a Global People workers' meeting," he continued. "We'll be going to a secret location so I can't tell you anymore now. You just need to act like a tourist who's going for a meal somewhere."

"And what's happening Monday?" I asked, "When you've left the country?"

"You'll be teaching at a house church – Ruth will organize that for you," he spoke quietly, so as not to be overheard.

I wondered who Ruth was – had I met her yet?

"You'll be at the house church for two days only and then Esther will arrange for you to travel to Vinh Long."

Ah! I knew who Esther was, I'd met her at the CMS church!

So on Saturday morning I did the tourist thing and took a coach trip to see a Buddhist shrine and visited a Chinese Market. I also visited the War Museum. I didn't really want to but went because Simon recommended it. It was almost unbelievable, the things that were done to the Vietnamese. I couldn't quite believe that humans could do such horrendous things to each other. I followed the pictures of a journalist who stayed for most of the war and got to go everywhere, taking pictures of atrocities and death. The thing that disturbed me most was that people would be hiding in little caves or tunnels and they would get blocked in and either the place would be set on fire or they would get blown up.

I walked out of the museum in stunned disbelief. Looking at the sea of Vietnamese people around me I suddenly realised that each of them either had a personal memory of the war or a memory passed down from generations before them. And, the thought hit me like a blow, these dreadful things happened right here, right beneath my feet.

SECRET ROOM

"He will call upon me, and I will answer him; I will be with him in trouble, I will deliver him and honour him."
(Psalm 91:15)

On Sunday, Simon and I went to one of the tourist areas of Ho Chi Minh City and walked along the streets looking for the restaurant where our secret meeting would be held.

"We can't arrive all together," Simon was explaining to me. "We have to enter the restaurant one at a time, though we, as tourists, can walk in together."

"Are there a lot of people going to this meeting?" I enquired.

"Yes, all the workers for Global People in the city."

I wondered how long it would take for us all to assemble. It was early afternoon and the day was bright and humid. At length we arrived at a garden bordered by a fence with a gate in it. There were Vietnamese people at the gate who greeted us and we walked through the garden towards a large restaurant. Red and white paint adorned the exterior and we passed under a veranda to enter the restaurant. I think the place must have been owned by a Christian because no one questioned us at all. We walked through the dining area towards the back of the building. At the tables real tourists were eating and talking and there was a lovely smell of cooking food. We walked up a narrow corridor and Simon suddenly stopped. He pressed his hand against a panel and a door swung inwards. We passed through and entered a sealed room.

The first thing that struck me was the smell. Something was cooking over a low flame in the middle of the room on a table and the stench from it was overpowering. There were people sitting around the table and they invited us to take the last two chairs. I sat down next to Simon and stared at the thing cooking in the pot over the flame. The thing glistened in the low light, its smooth surface appearing revolting to my western eyes.

"We have uterus to eat for lunch," one of the women said. "We hope that doesn't offend you."

I swallowed hard and said nothing whilst Simon murmured something positive. He must have seen the expression on my face and whispered:

"You'll have to eat some of it, otherwise they'll be offended."

As the meal was not yet ready, we prayed and the meeting began. Looking around I saw several people I recognised, including Esther from the CMS church as well as David the Global People co-ordinator. We prayed a bit more, this time for the general work of Global People and then the meal was served.

Simon, being diplomatic, took a large portion of the uterus and also placed a small bit on my plate. I hid most of it under my salad as I couldn't bear to look at it. I prayed, "Lord I'll keep it down if you will help me put it down," and God answered my prayer. When no-one was looking I wrapped the piece of uterus in my paper hanky and put it in my pocket! Knowing it was in my pocket was only slightly better than seeing it on my plate. Then I tucked into my salad and rice with gusto.

After the main course we continued with the meeting. It was very much like a business meeting with everyone there sharing successes and failures. Some of the street children workers were there and their reports were very encouraging. I also met Ruth who was to take me to the house church the following day. Ruth reported on the training she carried out on a regular basis. The people there also discussed translations into Vietnamese of various publications.

Although the meeting had been encouraging to both Simon and me, it was a relief, when after two hours in that stifling room, the meeting finished and we were allowed to leave. Apparently people could leave in groups this time. Simon and I walked through the garden and out onto the road. I breathed in the humid air gratefully, expelling the stench of cooked uterus from my lungs. As soon as we'd turned the corner I gingerly took the paper hanky out of my pocket and dropped the piece of uterus on the ground. I didn't think I wanted to know which animal it had come from.

THE CHURCH IN THE ROOF

"With long life will I satisfy him and show him my salvation." (Psalm 91:16)

Simon left Ho Chi Minh City on the Monday morning but I didn't see him before I left for my next assignment. Ruth, whom I had met the previous day picked me up on her motorbike and soon we were in the rush hour traffic. Although I was somewhat used to the chaos by now, I still found the travelling scary. We travelled roads I'd not been driven down and soon the landscape around me was completely unfamiliar. Then we reached the river. I found out afterwards that this was the river Saigon. All I knew at that point was that the river was as wide as the Severn and spanning it was a slender bridge. Clasping my holdall firmly, I gripped Ruth's jacket more tightly.

Once we were travelling over the bridge I discovered that the road was two lanes wide but the speed at which we were travelling was terrifying. Both lanes were thick with motorbikes and in some ways it was worse than town traffic as the flow of traffic went in both directions. Ruth was driving near the side

Travelling in Ho Chi Minh City

of the bridge where there were railings at regular intervals. I was tempted to grab hold of the railings as we passed them but stopped myself in time, realising that wouldn't be very sensible.

At last we were over the bridge and entering the Nhuan district. I knew that the house church was located somewhere across the river and relaxed a little as I realised the journey was nearly over. In a street of tall houses we stopped outside one nondescript looking place and parked the motorbike. As I followed Ruth into the house I noticed the silent watchers opposite the house and along the street. A shiver ran over my skin as I was reminded again of the risk we were all running.

All I knew about Ruth was that she was married to a pastor and that she conducted training courses regularly. She was here to learn from me today and I had hoped to get to know her a bit better but there was no time. Ruth took me to a room with a rope ladder hanging down from a trap door in the ceiling and indicated that I had to climb it. Slinging my holdall across my shoulders I was thankful for the Vietnamese preference for trousers – I would never have got up the ladder wearing a dress! I was slow to climb because of my hip and the ladder moved a lot. At last I was at floor level and hauled myself onto solid ground again.

Ruth appeared behind me as I was looking around for the people to train. The pastor's wife pointed above me and I saw with a sinking heart another rope ladder and trapdoor. I sighed, readjusted my holdall and started climbing again. By the time I reached the top I was sweating freely and the heat was rising. I was relieved to see a room full of people when my head reached floor level again. When Ruth appeared she counted the people in the room and then announced there was one more person to arrive. As we settled ourselves I discovered that some people had been here for hours already. They had been arriving since dawn, one at a time.

We were in a windowless room at the top of the house. To one side there were metal bowls of varying sizes stacked against the wall. Looking around I realised that there were no toilets, this was it for the next eight and a half hours! Such precautions were necessary when these Christians met together. House churches were not recognised or permitted by the government and these Christians daily ran the risk of prison and torture because of what they believed.

The last person arrived and someone in the house closed the trap door, sealing us in. Already it was hot and humid. I began training at 8.30 am and went on until 11.30 am. As at the CMS Church we stopped for lunch then and the metal bowls were brought into the centre of the room and opened. Each bowl contained some kind of food. I took mainly rice and vegetables. There was some meat but I heard someone say something about rats and decided to avoid it. There was also a fish dish but I had no desire to have a repeat performance of food poisoning again.

As we ate lunch together I noticed that one of the ladies was wearing a dress. This was so unusual that I asked Ruth about it.

"She is pregnant," the pastor's wife informed me. "When a woman is pregnant she wears a dress to indicate she is expecting."

Wearing a dress was probably cooler too, I thought to myself. We settled down to sleep just after noon and woke again by 1.30 pm in order to continue training. The heat was uncomfortable and the air was very stale by the time we finished at 5.30 pm. But as I taught and trained these people I realised how strong their faith was and saw how the persecution actually strengthened their resolve and love for God.

Altogether I spent two days at the Church in the Roof and saw how their strategy for training worked. It wasn't about asking foreign missionaries to come in – that was forbidden by the government. Instead, the indigenous Christians were missionaries to their own people. But in order to be trained they had to ask for outside help. That's where Simon and I came in and trained them.

On Wednesday evening, when Ruth dropped me back at Hotel Quang she told me quietly that Esther would meet me in the morning and catch a bus with me to Vinh Long.

VINH LONG

His faithfulness will be your shield and rampart. (Psalm 91:4b)

The bus rattled along the dusty roads, passing rice fields and rushing through villages and towns. Wherever there was water there were floating markets with vendors selling coconuts and many different kinds of fruit. It was Wednesday and I was on my way to Vinh Long with Esther and Rachel, a friend of hers. But I was sitting apart from them, pretending I didn't know them. This was all part of my tourist disguise – I didn't know anyone in Vietnam at all. I watched Esther and her friend sur-reptitiously, waiting for them to make a move so that I would know when to leave the bus. The bus was crowded and overly hot but it was good to relax, to watch the scenery pass by. I wasn't sure exactly what was happening once I was in Vinh Long, but I trusted Esther to get a message to me somehow.

We arrived in Vinh Long in the evening and I followed Esther and Rachel to the hotel where we were all staying. I waited for Esther to book in and, ignoring them totally, pre-tended to be a first-time tourist in Vietnam, which was the absolute truth! I unpacked my clothes in my room and sorted out some of my training materials. I knew I would only be here for a couple of days and Hotel Quang were keeping my room there free for me when I returned. As I was unpacking, I noticed Esther going for a walk, away from the hotel and wondered again what I should do next.

I didn't have to wonder for long. I had just finished supper at the restaurant next door to the hotel, when several motor-bikes pulled up outside. Paying for my meal I wandered out, thinking about getting an early night, when one of the ladies on the motorbikes approached me.

"Would you like to see the town?" she asked, smiling at me. "It's a free ride!"

I considered, looking around for Esther.

The lady spoke again, more quietly. "Esther told me you were here. I will be taking you to your meetings over the next couple of days. My name is Rebecca!"

I knew immediately that she was telling the truth and accepted her offer of a guided tour of Vinh Long by motor-bike. As we set off, I noticed Esther and her friend Rachel being offered lifts by other motorbike riders and together we were driven around the town. By now it was pitch dark but the town was lit by a myriad of lights. The thing that stands out most clearly in my memory are the motorbikes stopping on the famous bridge on the outskirts of Vinh Long.

"This was erected by New Zealanders," my guide told me.

We rested there for a while and I took a number of photos from the bridge of the lights and night sky line. I learnt that Rebecca had a teenage family and that she too was married to a pastor. Driving back to the hotel in the early hours of the morning, I noticed that there were still people eating outside small cafés.

"I will pick you up at 7.30 am," Rebecca whispered to me as I got off the motorbike.

Despite a lack of sleep, I woke feeling refreshed the next morning. Remembering that I was going to be picked up at 7.30 am I went in search of breakfast as soon as I had dressed. Returning to the restaurant next door to the hotel, I was disappointed. Breakfast appeared to be meat and noodles so I asked for some bread not wanting to face meat first thing in the morning!

RIVERS, BRIDGES AND PINK DUST ROADS

For he will command his angels concerning you to guard you in all your ways; they will lift you up in their hands, so that you will not strike your foot against a stone. (Psalm 91:11–12)

Seated behind Rebecca we drove through Vinh Long to the country, on our way to a secret destination. At regular intervals great, white monstrosities of stone reared their heads up in the rice fields. I learnt later that they were either monuments to people who had died in the war or just grave markers. I thought they spoiled the landscape!

We soon reached the Mekong River and my belly started twisting as though it had snakes dancing inside it. The Mekong River was vast and I could only just see the opposite shore. Rebecca indicated that we should dismount and wait for the ferry which was even now approaching. I looked around, aware of a lot of noise nearby. To one side was a floating market, similar to those I had seen yesterday on my way up to Vinh Long. Tall stilts jutted out into the river and around the platforms bobbed many boats filled with fruit and vegetables. All the boatmen were hawking their wares, wearing their conical hats and selling their goods to the customers who hurried backwards and forwards.

The ferry discharged its passengers and we climbed aboard, with the motorbike. There were a few other passengers with us in this flat bottomed craft and the ferryman pushed away from the bank. Apparently his was a busy trade too and he ferried people back and forth from dawn until dusk. The "snakes" in my belly still writhed as we crossed the river but the water was calm so I managed to relax a little. The river was a dirty colour and smelt strongly. But it wasn't overpowering and I enjoyed watching the birds flying over and around us. Despite the shore seeming far away, the crossing only took twenty minutes. Once on the other side, Rebecca and I got back onto the motorbike and set off again.

We were now on an island and followed a pink dust road through a tropical jungle. The road was compacted dust and only just wide enough for one car to drive down. In every direction all the eye could see was greenery. The narrow road cut a pink swathe through tall palms and dense tropical plants. Their shadows were black and cool across the path contrasting with the heat of the sun in the relatively open spaces. We passed only a handful of people and the occasional motorbike in half an hour. There were several houses miles apart from each other, set back off the road. The humidity was rising as we progressed and I began to feel exceedingly hot and sticky. The snakes in my belly had vanished however, and I was enjoying the beautiful scenery around me.

Then we arrived at a bridge and Rebecca slowed the motor-bike down, turning her head towards me.

"Estuary of the Mekong River!" I thought I heard her say.

At once the snakes were back in my belly with a vengeance. The bridge appeared to be made of wood and looked very unsafe. It was not very wide with only a low rail on either side and the sight of it filled me with fear. *I can't swim!* I thought to myself. *If we fall over the edge, I'm done for!* We drove onto the bridge and I clung to Rebecca's waist for dear life. I knew I was a lot heavier than the driver and surely the bridges had been made for the little Vietnamese people, not people twice their size.

I made the mistake of looking over the edge to see how near the river water was. I thought my heart had jumped out of my chest and that the "snakes" in my belly were trying to race after it. The river was thirty foot below us! From up on the bridge the water appeared placid but that was small comfort. I learnt later that the Mekong River had many estuaries and that it was quite normal to have these high bridges all over the country. The bridge was not long and I heaved a ragged sigh of relief once we were back on the pink dust road.

Shortly after the high bridge however, we had to stop again. The road ended and Rebecca parked her motorbike in the shade by yet another estuary of the Mekong. A ferry was waiting on our side of the bank and at our approach the ferryman pushed his boat into the river. My stomach lurched as the water slapped the sides of the boat. Unlike the main Mekong River, this estuary was choppy and wild. I sat there swallowing against the rising sickness and noticed as I stared fixedly at the front of the ferry that water was slowly leaking in through the sides. Shifting my gaze around the boat I discovered that water was seeping through the joints all over the place. I couldn't work out if it was fear I was feeling or just normal water sickness.

My legs were shaky when we arrived on the far bank and Rebecca led me along a normal earthen coloured road. The vegetation was not as thick and tropical as it had been and after a short while we arrived at an unofficial church. The building was quite ornate and nearby was someone's dwelling place. There was also a large covered area where tall, wide pots stood and cauldrons hung over small fires. There were a number of people around, tending the pots, preparing the meals for the day. There was also a place to shower which I thought quite necessary as my clothes was soaked and my hair was plastered to my head. After such a traumatic journey I asked for the toilet and was shown to a brick building set back from the house. Although it wasn't a flush toilet, it was very clean.

It was now just before 9.00 am and I started training straightaway. Every time I moved to demonstrate something I was aware of water running down my face and down my back. There were between seventy and eighty students, including Esther and Rachel who had arrived separately from Rebecca and me. I was struck again at how fearless these Christians were. They were very gentle and totally unphased by the fact that the secret police could raid the meetings at any moment. They laughed readily and were eager to learn. Always smiling, they knew how to have fun and they were totally committed to following Jesus. The students came from a wide area and some of them took turns in watching for the secret police.

We stopped at 11.30 am as usual and moved from the church building to the covered area to have lunch. Eating around the cauldrons we helped ourselves to food from lots of little metal pots. There was rice and noodles and a little meat. There was also some gravy-like substance and green vegetables including bean shoots. After teaching in the afternoon until 4.00 pm, I left with Rebecca. As we walked to the ferry I wished that I could have stayed at the church. I was not looking forward to the journey back to Vinh Long. Although the fear of water did not go away, I found that each time I travelled either by water or over water, God gave me strength not to panic. Every step of the journey that day and the next was a battle but it made me more aware of God's grace and love for me.

SECRET POLICE

Surely he will save you from the fowler's snare and from the deadly pestilence. (Psalm 91:3)

I spent Friday at the same church, teaching the same people. On the Saturday, however, Rebecca waited by the second ferry for Esther and Rachel to arrive. Then we took a different path and walked for a long time until we reached a secret garden. Here I met different people, all from the underground church. We started off with a time of intense worship and prayer. Then I taught all morning. Surrounded by a sea of colour – one woman wore pink trousers – and avid listeners, I forgot the time. It was only when my stomach growled that I realised I was hungry. Glancing at my watch I saw that it was midday already.

Just then there was a disturbance at the back of the crowd listening to me. A woman, red faced and dishevelled, panting as if she had been running was talking quietly but urgently to the men around her. Everyone rose to their feet and people started to disappear in all directions. No-one panicked, everyone was very controlled, as if they had done this many times before. Wondering what was going on, I saw Esther and Rachel slip away. Then Rebecca was at my side, handing me my bag and pulling me after her.

"Come with me now," was all she said.

Thoughts of the secret police flashed through my mind. I knew that these people's lives depended on my obedience and

I followed Rebecca without a word. We took the path we'd walked earlier and Rebecca set the pace, neither quick or slow. Her face was composed and she looked like someone taking a tourist for a walk. I fell into character and gawped at the vegetation around us. I didn't think it would be right to stop for photos though. A sense of urgency filled me and I had to restrain myself from speeding up. We passed several people on the road and I looked at each one of them, wondering if they were the secret police. There was no way of knowing. For all I knew the secret police could have been approaching from any direction.

When we reached the river bank the ferry was on the other side, so we sat down to wait. Quietly, Rebecca told me what was going on.

"The woman who turned up who had been running," she whispered. "That was a pastor's wife of a church in the area. The pastor, his wife and another member of their church were caught earlier on today for openly telling people about Jesus. The secret police put them in prison and somehow the pastor's wife managed to escape. She had no idea you were to be speaking at the secret garden, otherwise she would have gone elsewhere for refuge. She thought she had been followed so we all had to leave immediately."

I felt quite shaken and prayed that all the Christians I'd been with that morning would get home safely. It was my only brush with the secret police and even that slight experience was terrifying.

The ferry arrived then and we got aboard. It was still leaking water I noticed as my stomach started to writhe like snakes. The water was even more choppy than usual and the punt (I didn't really think of it as a proper ferry), began to rock, quite dangerously to my mind. The ferryman carried on poling us across the river as normal, seemingly totally unaware of the danger to his passengers. The motion got worse and the water started splashing over the sides of the boat. In a panic I flung my arms around the ferryman, holding onto him to try and make him calm the boat's motion down. This only made things worse and we rocked from side to side. I suddenly realised we must look like something out of a pantomime and Rebecca disentangled me from the ferryman, making me sit down again.

We reached the far bank without any more panics and Rebecca then took me back to my hotel.

"I think you should leave for Ho Chi Minh City today," she said as I thanked her for looking after me. "I will go and have a word with Esther. You go and eat and then pack."

LEAVING VIETNAM

You will tread upon the lion and the cobra; you will trample the great lion and the serpent. (Psalm 91:13)

Later that afternoon when I had eaten and packed my belongings, I checked out of the hotel and waited for a bus, pretending I still didn't know Esther and Rachel who were standing nearby. The bus, when it arrived, was nearly full. I thought I had found a seat to myself but at the last minute a Vietnamese lady hurried aboard and sat down next to me. She was very chatty and the journey passed quickly as the daylight faded. We talked about teaching as I had been a teacher and she had just been teaching in Vinh Long. She was now returning to Ho Chi Minh City to take up a teaching post there. I told her about the teaching system in England, hiding behind my tourist disguise, and she was very interested in what I told her. In return she told me about teaching methods in Vietnam and how it was very hard work being a teacher. The Vietnamese children attend school from 6.00 am until 1.00 pm and then they come back from 2.00 pm until 8.00 pm. Reaching Hotel

Quang late that night I slept well, exhausted by the events of the day and the journey.

On Sunday Esther picked me up on her motorbike and we went to a church I hadn't yet visited. I sat at the back and discovered there were headphones in the pews. Putting my set of headphones on, I heard the Vietnamese sermon being translated into English for me!

On the way back to the hotel after breakfast on Monday I noticed a sign for tourist trips to several islands nearby. I enquired as to which island I could visit that morning and was told there was a trip arranged to the island of Ben Hur. So at mid-morning I found myself waiting for a coach with a large group of other tourists from various countries. The coach trip to the island took about an hour and when we arrived at the River Mekong, there was a boat waiting to take us across the water. This boat was very different from the ferries I'd travelled in recently. There were no leaks and the motion was actually quite comfortable. I got the impression that some boats were only used for tourist trips and nothing else.

Ben Hur itself was a small island full of lush vegetation. I wandered around the island with the other tourists, enjoying the pleasant atmosphere and gazing up at the tall coconut palms. We followed winding dust paths, taking photos of the plants that to my mind looked almost tropical. In several parts of the island there were Vietnamese people working and we watched them. They took coconut shells and carved and painted them, creating souvenirs that I had seen in the gift shops in Ho Cho Minh City. Everything they used was natural and they obviously enjoyed their work.

As we made our way back to where the chartered boat was waiting for us, we saw a crowd of people laughing and pointing. Intrigued, we hurried over to the crowd to see what was happening. To my horror I saw a very large snake being handled by several Vietnamese. Before I could turn away, one of the men caught my eye and offered to take a photo of me holding the snake. I started to refuse as everyone around encouraged me to take up the offer. Hesitating I looked at the large, mud coloured serpent who stared coldly back at me, its forked tongue flickering in and out. I didn't want to be seen as a wimpy English woman, especially around all these international tourists and reluctantly agreed.

Handing over my camera to a bystander, I walked up to the man holding the snake.

"Is vegetarian!" he whispered to me, grinning.

I smiled weakly at him. That was a small comfort. He guided the snake onto my arm and I let it glide up behind my neck and down my other arm. It felt heavy and firm and my neck bowed under its weight. I couldn't help feeling shivers of revulsion running down my back and struggled with a smile for the photo. As quickly as I could, I handed the creature back, regained possession of my camera and retreated, hoping we would be called aboard the boat very soon.

In the evening I returned to my hotel and was sorting out the materials I wanted to leave behind and wondering how I could do this. My problem was solved for me the following day as I had a stream of visitors. My contacts such as Judith, Esther, Rachel and Ruth as well as other women I had met the week before, came to visit me one at a time. Each one brought me a little present and each one had a different excuse for visiting me such as to tell me something, to ask for something or to get something photocopied. I was a bit puzzled at the gifts because I had intended to leave all my training materials here in Vietnam anyway. It was an odd day and by the end of it I was feeling exhausted and had developed a cough.

The cough was worse on the Wednesday morning when I flew from Ho Chi Minh City to Bangkok and then to Bangladesh for further training sessions. I coughed throughout the flight and an American sitting near me remarked that I had legionnaires' disease. I just smiled at him. I knew I hadn't got that! But I was a bit concerned about how the cough would affect my speech in Dacca. Then I fell to pondering my trip to Vietnam.

When I had been weak, God had been strong, I thought, remembering the first day of training after recovering from food poisoning. I had known that I could depend on God in any situation but this trip had really brought that home to me. I felt as though my trust in God was greater because of both the good and the bad situations I'd been in. And best of all, I didn't think I'd got any of the underground Christians in to trouble due to my association with them!

Myanmar Missionaries

MYANMAR

They are armed with bow and spear, they are cruel and show no mercy . . . I have made you a tester of metals and my people the ore, that you may observe and test their ways. (Jeremiah 6:23, 27)

Myanmar, previously known as Burma, is situated in South-East Asia, bordered to the west by India, to the north by China and with Laos and Thailand on its eastern flank. The country also borders the Andaman Sea and Bay of Bengal. The population of approximately 50 million live in the 261,288 square miles that once was an independent kingdom. Burma was annexed to the colony of India by the British Empire in 1886 and briefly occupied by the Japanese during the Second World War. The country returned to British rule after the war and later the rule passed to the military junta. Although the military government was recognised by the United Nations, some countries refused to acknowledge the new government and still refuse to recognise the new name Myanmar. Much of the Burmese population do not call their country Myanmar as they too refuse to acknowledge the military junta. The official language is still Burmese and the population generally consider themselves to be Burmese. Literacy education is poor with only thirty per cent of the population being able to read. The currency is the kyat but US dollars are also valued currency. The kyat is not available outside of Myanmar.

The terrain is a mixture of hills and valleys, bordered by mountains to the north, east and west. Within the mountain barriers lie the flat lands of Ayeyarwaddy, Chindwin and Sittaung River valleys. The wide, flat paddy fields are drenched in water during the summer season. Tropical forests

89.2 per cent of the population are Buddhist

cover the flanks of the hills and mountains that appear to just rise up out of the vast plains. The tops of the mountains are blunt, rocky protrusions, appearing other-worldly through the constant heat haze that turns the distance blue. The cities are lushly populated with tropical trees and plants. Out of the sea of dark green foliage rise the white domes and golden spires of Buddhist temples. During the summer, the atmosphere is hot with high humidity and rain during June to September. Winter is less cloudy with scant rainfall and lower humidity.

In 1966 the communist military government expelled all known Christians and the country was closed to foreign missionaries and any active Christian movement. The Christians had not broken any law or done anything to warrant being expelled from their homeland. Instead, the government had come to see Christians as independent thinkers and decided that if there were too many of them, they could easily challenge the government. The doors were firmly closed to

Christianity and the communist government ruled the country through the military, controlling the people by force.

Today, 89.2 per cent of the population are Buddhist, with only 5 per cent of the population professing to be Christian. The other 5.8 per cent are a mixture of Islam, Hinduism and Spiritualism. Although rich in natural resources such as timber, tin, zinc, copper, lead, coal and precious stones, Myanmar is currently the world's largest producer of heroin. The country employs four million child labourers in its industries and the sex trade is growing rapidly. AIDS is set to explode in the population.

Nearly forty years after the government expelled the Christians, there is still a church in Myanmar. The Christians are very restricted as to what they are allowed to do. Evangelism is prohibited and financial help for church buildings is not forthcoming from the government. Outside financial help is forbidden. All Christians are allowed to do is to meet in their church buildings. They are not even allowed to talk about the Holy Spirit. Due to the poor economy the church buildings are often in a state of disrepair.

Ten per cent of the population lives in Yangon, formerly Rangoon, which is Myanmar's capital city, situated in the southernmost part of the country. In 1988 there was a student uprising in Yangon. In protest against the controlling government, the students climbed the trees in the main square and shot at the soldiers sent to arrest them. The students had bows and arrows, the soldiers had guns. The army successfully put down the uprising and, to prevent such a thing happening again, the government ordered the trees in the square to be cut down.

This was the atmosphere I was facing as I prepared to visit Myanmar in July 2003. I was well aware that the country was one of the most dangerous places to share the gospel and had read reports that made the persecutions in Vietnam seem mild. No evangelistic Christianity, no foreign money, no foreign missionaries allowed – and I was preparing to break all the rules.

BANGKOK – WHICH KFC?

For this God is our god for ever and ever; he will be our guide even to the end. (Psalm 48:14)

World Gospel had invited me to Myanmar to provide training for the Christians there. I was to travel with a girl from Nagaland, (the mountainous area where India meets Myanmar), who had been in Myanmar before with World Gospel. Not long before I was due to fly out, I received an email from Susannah who was to be my travelling companion and co-trainer, suggesting we meet in Bangkok at the KFC on the ground floor. Global People, a branch of World Gospel had also asked me to take some money out to Myanmar that was to be used for Christian projects. They transferred the amount I was to take and I drew it out of my bank account in US dollars before I left England.

I was no stranger to Bangkok airport, having changed planes there for Vietnam the previous year. I hadn't noticed a KFC before and stared around at the shops and terminals, feeling a bit lost. The airport was like a city itself and was built on many levels. I knew where I had to go in order to catch the plane to Yangon and not wanting to get myself lost, I approached an airport official.

"Excuse me," I said, "Can you tell me where the KFC is located?"

The dark skinned man stared up at me and frowned. "There are three KFCs in this airport."

That floored me. I racked my brains, trying to remember what Susannah's email had said. "It's the one on the ground floor I think. How do I reach it?"

The airport official frowned again. "That KFC is outside the airport. You will need a visa."

I hadn't expected this at all. "How much will a visa cost?" I asked.

It turned out the visa would cost the equivalent of £35 and my heart sank. Thanking the official for his help I stood in the middle of the crowds, wondering what to do. People of every shape and colour swarmed around me, making a deafening noise and assailing my nostrils with a variety of odours. I could have paid for the visa as I was carrying a lot of money in my case. But the problem was, only a small proportion of the money was actually mine and I wanted to use it for expenses in Myanmar. In the end I decided not to pay out and took my luggage to the waiting area by the terminal for my flight to Yangon.

"Lord," I prayed as I sat down and waited, "You'll just have to bring Susannah and me together."

Arriving at the terminal as early as I did I had a long wait. But I didn't mind. I knew God would bring Susannah to me in time for the flight. I arranged my poncho around me, trying to look casual and watched the never-ending flow of humanity, amazed at the variety in skin tone and facial features that passed me.

Eventually Susannah arrived. Neither of us knew what the other looked like but as soon as she came through the barrier into the waiting area, I recognised her. For some reason she stood out from the masses around us. There was no distinguishing mark or feature about her. I just saw this dark skinned woman walk through the barrier. She was medium height and medium build, with long, dark hair. She was wearing a pretty blue blouse and I caught her eye and just knew it was Susannah. I smiled at her and she smiled back, walking over to me. Sitting down next to me she asked;

"Are you Monica?"

"I am. You must be Susannah."

She smiled again and I had the impression of someone who was very friendly and easygoing.

"I like your blouse," I commented.

"Thank you. I bought it today, here in Bangkok."

"Sorry, but I couldn't come to the KFC," I said. "I needed a visa to get to it."

Susannah shrugged. "We've met up anyway."

I relaxed and thanked God silently for answering my prayer.

As we walked onto the plane I felt as though every eye was on my hand luggage. I wasn't too worried about my main suitcase as that only had a bit of money hidden in it. But in my hand luggage, on the either hand, I was carrying nearly Six and a half thousand US dollars. Susannah and I found our seats and the plane took off. Once we'd levelled out I made my excuses and walked to the toilet. Susannah smiled as I left my seat; she knew what I was about to do.

Once safely locked inside the toilet I took off my poncho and undid my bag. The crisp dollar notes stared at me accusingly. What I was about to do was deceitful. Resolutely I tucked the first wad inside the waistband of my trousers. Swiftly I packed the money around my middle, fastened my trousers securely and slipped my poncho back on. I had about one and a half thousand US dollars left in my hand luggage, which I couldn't conceal on my body. I was aware that it might seem a bit odd for me to be carrying so much money in my hand luggage but decided to say, if asked, that I thought it would be safer there. Smoothing my hair down I flushed the toilet and returned to my seat. Susannah said nothing, but I felt as though I was crackling with the amount of paper around my waist. I was also getting very hot but couldn't work out if that was the change in temperature or increased nervousness on my part.

I knew that the Myanmar authorities were very strict on how much money tourists were allowed to take in and out of the country. This was to ensure that the people of Myanmar couldn't leave their country without permission. There were very strict rules about where the people could go and for how long. I had been asked to take in money for twelve projects for the Christians there and I obviously couldn't declare I had so much money on me. The limit for a tourist was two thousand US dollars. If you had more than that amount, your passport was stamped and you then had to declare how much you'd spent when you left the country and provide receipts as proof. This effectively prevented foreigners from giving handouts to the people. There was no way I could declare I was bringing US$6.5k into Myanmar because I intended to give it away to the people who needed it.

To take my mind off what I was doing I talked to Susannah. She had been to Myanmar before with World Gospel and told me a bit about the people I would be meeting. I learnt a little about Susannah herself. She was in her early forties and was from a high caste family. Recently she had been a headmistress at a Christian school in Nagaland.

YANGON AIRPORT

Rescue me, O Lord, from evil men; protect me from men of violence. (Psalm 140:1)

My first impression as I stepped off the plane at Yangon was of many soldiers and guns. The army was everywhere dressed in khaki coloured uniforms, carrying their guns quite openly. The atmosphere was tense and I broke out in a sweat. We picked up our luggage and were given a piece of paper each to sign. Mine was a declaration in English that I wasn't bringing more than two thousand US dollars into the country. I hesitated and didn't tick the box that would incriminate me, handing the sheet of paper back to the official. Immediately, I felt dreadfully guilty and cold sweat trickled down my back.

As Susannah and I lined up in different queues to have our luggage searched, I recalled an incident some years in the past. Back in England I had taken an elderly gentleman to his home in Camber after a meeting at Shell House. The evening was closing in as I returned to Hastings via Rye. As I approached Freda Gardham School I noticed a police car parked at the side of the road. Drawing abreast of the police car I realised the policeman standing beside it was holding a speed gun. I didn't think any more of it until the blue lights flashed in my rear view mirror and I was pulled over. I had forgotten that the speed limit suddenly changed to thirty mph near the School and apparently I had been doing fifty-two mph. I hadn't intended to break the law but I was fined £40. At that time I was living by faith on about £4 a week but in the next couple of days someone who knew nothing of the incident gave me the money to pay the fine.

But here I was now in Myanmar about to break the law quite deliberately. It seemed such a paradox. I hoped God would protect me and tried not to think of the consequences if they searched me. I noticed Susannah's queue was moving faster than my own and watched her hand luggage being searched. Then she was waved on and I saw her wait for me at the entrance to the airport. I felt more and more uptight and had lost that peaceful feeling that I was so used to. My faith was at sub zero level and I could feel hot and cold sweats break out all over me nearly every minute. I had nearly reached the table where everyone's luggage was searched and the lady in front of me was still waiting. Airport officials were inspecting her suitcase when another official beckoned me over to have my passport checked.

Cold lumps of dread congealed in my stomach and I thought, "Here comes the crunch!" Just then a thought came into my head that I should look confident. Instead of looking as though

I had something to hide, I should act as if I was one hundred per cent tourist. The peace I associated with God's voice flooded back into me and I stood up straight. I marched over to the desk with my luggage, trying to ignore the number of soldiers standing to attention with guns ready to use. I showed my passport to the official and inside I was still thinking about what excuse I could give if all the money was discovered.

The lady in front of me still had her suitcase wide open and an official was searching through the interior with his torch. I concentrated on looking confident. I wouldn't really have any excuse for taking all the American money into the country. I couldn't even say that I didn't understand the form I'd been given as it had been written in English. The official examined my passport carefully and I eyed the metal detectors a few feet away with a certain amount of trepidation. Due to my hip replacement I always seemed to set alarms off. I really hoped that wouldn't happen this time as I didn't want to draw any attention to myself.

The official handed my passport back to me and I smiled at him as I went to put my luggage on the desk. But the man shook his head and waved me through. Heart beating wildly, I could hardly believe it as I walked past the metal detectors without setting them off and joined Susannah at the entrance. My legs were quite shaky with relief as I realised God had made me almost invisible. The officials were still going through the other lady's suitcase as we left the airport.

Outside it was dark and humid. Two Christians whom Susannah recognised from her visit before, met us. Anna and her husband Justin headed up a church in Yangon and would be acting as translators during our training sessions. They were both short and had open, smiling faces. They were obviously very pleased to see both of us and made us feel very welcome. They talked a lot to Susannah as she had met them before and arranged for a taxi to take us all to our hotel. I sank into the taxi seat with relief, feeling exhausted but triumphant that I'd got through the official checks and still had all the money I'd been entrusted with.

YANGON

. . . ruthless men seek my life – men without regard for God. (Psalm 54:3)

As Susannah and I were posing as tourists we had to stay at a hotel. The drive from the airport only took about twenty minutes. The hotel had a bland name that I have since forgotten but it was nice and modern, and the staff were very friendly. Anna and Justin were extremely helpful. They carried our luggage into the hotel for us and helped us find our room. When the hotel staff had left, Justin closed the door and Anna slipped an empty bag off her shoulder. Justin stood with his back against the door and nodded.

"Monica, do you have the money?" Anna asked me.

I couldn't wait to get rid of it and hurried to the bathroom. Susannah helped Anna pack the money into her bag whilst Justin listened out for staff coming back. I peeled the wads of notes from their hiding place around my waist and then opened my carry-all and handed over the rest. Once the money had been hidden in the bag, Anna searched in her pockets for a piece of paper, which she handed to me. This I concealed in my Bible, feeling greatly relieved. The piece of paper was a receipt that I needed to take back to World Gospel, to prove that I had delivered the money safely.

"We must go now," Anna announced, shouldering the bag. "We see you tomorrow!"

And with that she and Justin disappeared. Susannah and I were sharing a large room and that evening we only unpacked what we would need for that night and the next morning. I felt totally drained and Susannah appeared tired too. We looked at the menus in our rooms and realised we didn't know what to ask for. Susannah announced she wasn't hungry and decided she would go to bed early. I ordered a simple rice dish and struggled to eat it.

I felt as though I was in a hot bathroom. The atmosphere was over eighty-five per cent humidity and it felt far worse than Vietnam. The temperature was 40 °C and I felt as though I couldn't breathe. I knew I didn't have chest problems and realised it must have been the heat. It was as though something was constantly pressing on my chest so that my breathing was very shallow. I knew it was monsoon season but I hadn't realised it would be this bad!

Soon after I'd eaten I went to bed and although I was tired it took a while for me to fall asleep. I hoped the atmosphere would be less intense further inland where we were scheduled to provide training for teachers and children's leaders. I told myself that I only had to put up with this amount of humidity for twenty-four hours. My mind slowly turned over the notes I'd prepared for the seminars. I wouldn't be allowed to be directly involved with the children, but those I trained would pass the training on to others.

In the morning, Justin and Anna turned up to take us on a tour of Yangon. They brought with them their own taxi driver who was a Christian involved in the church that Justin headed up. Justin was also the co-ordinator for Global People so he had lots of interesting tales to tell Susannah and me as we were driven around the city.

I knew that Yangon had a population of about five million but hadn't really appreciated what that figure meant. The city seethed with humanity. Sunlight broke through the clouds and gleamed off the white and gold structures of the Buddhist temples. Although the trip was interesting and entertaining, I couldn't get away from that feeling of menace and fear that had struck me as soon as I had left the plane

Travelling in Yangon

the previous day. Several times we were stopped by soldiers who checked our passports. Soldiers were everywhere, walking, standing guard, stopping people and all of them had guns. Overhead there were helicopters constantly circling, the people inside them keeping a watch from above. As we travelled from place to place in Yangon I thought of the phrase in one of Paul's letters – "Our fight is not against flesh and blood . . .". There was something dreadfully sinister about the way everyone was constantly watched and checked. We had to be careful of what we said when there were other people about. One wrong word and all of us could have ended up in prison.

We had to pay the taxi driver at the end of the day and I was surprised at how expensive the fare was. But we had had a good day and I felt like a tourist! We had eaten during the day so we did not eat at the hotel in the evening. Instead, Susannah and I packed our bags and our Christian taxi driver drove us to Minglarden, which is just outside Yangon. We reached Minglarden just before 5.00 pm and met up with Justin and Anna who were accompanying us north to Meiktila.

The journey from Minglarden to Meiktila was considered long and we therefore had to travel by bus at night when it was relatively cooler. Justin and Anna paid for their seats first and, as I was waiting for Susannah to purchase her bus seat, Justin lent towards me and whispered:

"I think you'd better book two seats for yourself Monica!"

I thought he was joking and followed his gaze to the small seats available. The Burmese are small-boned and the seat area available for each person was tiny. I felt a bit embarrassed. Justin was right. There was no way my bottom was going to fit into a single seat. Susannah handed over her money and moved on up the aisle, following Justin and Anna to their seats. Reluctantly I requested two seats and the driver showed no surprise at all. Feeling rather flushed I stowed my luggage overhead and sat down, across two seats.

"Comfortable Monica?" asked Justin who was sitting behind me with his wife.

I turned and gave him a wry smile. Susannah had settled herself across the aisle from Justin and had already closed her eyes. The bus started up with a rattle and a bang and we were off. There were several stops on our way out into the country as the soldiers had frequent check points along the roads into the city. I showed my passport to various officials and then at last the journey began properly. To begin with I enjoyed the journey. We travelled north, past paddy fields of yellow, green and brown. Many of the rectangular fields were under water and clumps of dark green leaved tropical trees rose out of the plains. The trees broke up the chequer board effect, lending dimension and height to an otherwise flat landscape. Away in the distance rose brown, rocky hills, bare heads still reflecting the fierce sunlight. Every so often the bus stopped to take on board new passengers and the newcomers always stared at me, sitting across two seats!

When the sun had set however, darkness fell swiftly like a velvet glove, shrouding the paddy fields from view. I felt my eyes grow heavy and drifted in and out of sleep. The heat, though nowhere near as oppressive as it had been, was still uncomfortable and my sleep was light and broken.

MEIKTILA

I know what it is to be in need, and I know what it is to have plenty. I have learned the secret of being content in any and every situation, whether well fed or hungry, whether living in plenty or in want. (Philippians 4:12)

Our room at the hotel in Meiktila was small and humid. As we arrived there at five o'clock on Sunday morning, Susannah and I decided it wasn't worth going to bed. We'd had our passports checked several times on the road into Meiktila and were feeling a bit jittery, as though someone was watching us. So we unpacked our luggage and had some breakfast, being careful to talk about the usual tourist things – the weather and what sites we wanted to see. Susannah kept a look out for our lift, which had been organised in advance and we tried to give the hotel staff the impression that we were going out site-seeing early. At length our lift arrived, a young man in a noisy car.

"This is one of my contact's sons," Susannah shouted over the noise of the engine. "His father is a business man and he and his brothers help their father with the business."

Further conversation was impossible and we watched the streets pass by. The church in Meiktila had a church building that they called a Bible college. Opposite the college, was a white house, which was an orphanage. The walls were dirty

Orphans in Meiktila

white and there was a great pile of rubble near the gate. The building was quite a solid looking affair and the children appeared happy. Simply dressed in clothes that didn't quite fit them they posed and laughed as I took photos of them. The orphanage had its own water supply, which was pumped up from an underground water source. The orphans were present at the service in the church and they sang several songs to us. Occasionally the singing and preaching were drowned out by the sound of a helicopter flying overhead. Throughout the week the orphans vied for our attention whenever we appeared outside the church. Their smiling faces were there to welcome us in the mornings and to say goodbye to us when we left in the evenings.

On Monday morning we started training. I felt hot and dusty and my hair was lank and soaked in sweat. I had already had a cool shower and wished I'd had time to wash my hair but now it was 8.30 am and I was about to start training.

Christian teachers and children's leaders had assembled at the bible college for three days of intensive training. There were about 104 students altogether and each day our team taught them from 8.30 am until 9.00 pm. Once classes had finished, the students then spent their time in prayer and fellowship before catching a few hours sleep and returning for classes the following morning. One student told me how much she appreciated being able to spend so much time with other Christians.

Justin led the training and each of us women had different parts to play. Susannah provided some teaching and I discovered that the way I taught things was vastly different from anything they had experienced before. The previous training sessions these Christians had were quite subdued and cerebral. I knew nothing of this until afterwards when people were comparing my techniques to what they were used to.

I waltzed in there with my usual repartee, which is not strait-laced, or mechanical at all. For instance, I taught them how to teach memory verses using a dice. To do this I treated the students as children so that they could experience the method first hand. I divided my group of thirty into five smaller groups and numbered them one to five. The verse we were memorising was short, only five words long. Each group was given one of the words from the verse on a piece of paper, which was placed on the ground, face down. Then I threw a dice and called out a number and that particular group was allowed to turn over their word. When all the words had been turned over they then had to work out the word order and then learn the verse. It was a fun way of memorising a verse and easy too because the children could hear each word as it was turned over. They then became familiar with the words as they worked out the order in which they should go and then learning the verse was fairly easy!

The Burmese Christians loved my approach and I was quite taken aback at their enthusiasm for the games I got them playing, showing them how to make things fun for the children. They also enjoyed the different ways I got them to tell stories. It made them think beyond their usual methods and stretched their imaginations. When I wasn't teaching I watched Anna's training sessions with great interest. Although she was used to quite rigid ways of training, I noticed that she went beyond the outward proofs of leadership ability and probed deeper. She conducted most of her training in Burmese, whereas I had to be translated by Justin. I noticed she used drama a lot and at the end of each session she enabled her trainees to respond as themselves. I realised she was drawing out of them qualities such as compassion and mercy, rather than just giving them the authority to teach.

On our last day in Meiktila, I met the business man whose sons had been providing lifts for Susannah and me between the hotel and the church. Usually we had eaten lunch at the church and the meal normally lasted about an hour. On the Tuesday, however, we were driven to Barnabas' house. Barnabas was a Christian and very well off. Although he had no servants, he ran his own business selling wheels and parts for cars. He lived in a small house with his business at the back. We were shown into a long, narrow room with a coffee table in the centre and low seats arranged around the edges of the room. Barnabas' wife served us lunch and I found sitting on the low chairs quite interesting. It was very comfortable but, with my awkward hip, trying to get up out of the chairs was a bit difficult! Barnabas' wife looked radiant, even though she was the mother of his many children ranging from toddlers to teenagers.

The atmosphere was very friendly and jovial. Anna and Justin knew Barnabas very well and Susannah had met him on her previous trip to Myanmar. There was plenty of food and I filled my plate with cooked vegetables. The others ate meat and although it smelt good, I declined, not wanting to risk an upset stomach with another long bus journey to make the next day. The conversation revolved mainly around the church and what the Christians were doing in Meiktila. A few questions were asked about my background and history but I preferred to talk about the work we were doing here and now.

We returned to the church to finish our training and at the end Susannah and I decided to look around the town. I had taken some photos of the buildings and streets when Susannah suggested we go for a ride.

"Look! Let's take a pony and cart for a bit," she said. "I'll take a photo of you if you like."

I agreed and we paid the driver to take us a short distance. Climbing aboard the cart I suddenly realised how small the pony was. As I sat down the pony skittered and I had visions of my weight tipping the cart up on end and lifting the pony off its hooves.

"Smile Monica!" called Susannah and I forced a grimace.

I thought the pony was straining rather to draw the cart but Susannah and the driver didn't seem to notice that anything was amiss. As we rode along I noticed again how small and slight the Burmese were. No wonder I'd nearly tipped the pony off its hooves! At the end of the ride it was a short walk back to the hotel and we started packing for our next journey. That night, after supper, I lay in bed hearing rain pour down noisily. That was the first time I'd heard rain since we'd arrived in Myanmar. I wondered how badly the roads would be affected for our journey the following day.

MANDALAY

May the Lord answer you when you are in distress; may the name of the God of Jacob protect you. May he send you help from the sanctuary and grant you support from Zion. (Psalm 20:1–2)

On the Wednesday our small group left Meiktila for Mandalay. This bus trip was considered a "local" journey so we could travel there during the day. Again I bought two seats and endured the local people staring at me in surprise. *I can't help being larger than you!* I wanted to tell them, but remained silent. I was a tourist and should not draw attention to myself. There were the usual checks on the way out of Meiktila, with suspicious officials staring at me and comparing me to my passport photo. Their eyes occasionally ran over my luggage above my head and I felt as though they had X-ray eyes and could see my Bible and seminar notes. For some reason I thought a local journey only meant an hour or so and was quite surprised to realise after two hours on the bus that we were only halfway there!

We travelled north again, passing through beautiful countryside. I remember one valley of paddy fields with mountains all around them, like a basin. I was struck by the majesty of the mountains and the way the further ranges appeared lighter until they vanished in the heat haze. I noticed that a lot of the housing near the paddy fields was made of bamboo and almost always the houses were built near water. Often the houses were built on stilts and jutted out into wide, calm rivers. Due to the recent, heavy rain there was widespread flooding and many of the houses and animal huts had been knocked over. But as we travelled through this region I watched people carrying their houses and huts away from the water's edge to dry ground and erect them there. The house walls were generally made of woven bamboo so they must have been easy to relocate!

The scenery changed slowly and we left the valleys behind us, heading towards the cities in the middle of Myanmar. The road we were driving along was similar to a dual carriageway in England. We were driving on a single track and there was another single track in which vehicles were travelling in the opposite direction. In between the two tracks was a strip of land with cattle tethered to bushes. It seemed a paradox to have a dual carriageway but also to have grazing land for the animals between the two roads. Ox drawn carts lumbered up and down the tracks, carrying both people and materials.

There were more checks on the way into Mandalay by stern faced soldiers who seemed to take their duty very seriously. Even when we left the bus, I felt as though there were eyes everywhere, watching us.

Justin and Anna were staying at the same hotel as Susannah and I, for the first night. It was late when we arrived and the four of us were met at the bus stop by a couple who had organised the training in Mandalay. They organised a taxi to take all six of us to the hotel they had booked for us. The hotel looked like a tourist hotel and was therefore suitable for our disguise. It was more akin to a western hotel compared to some of the other places Susannah and I had stayed at. There was even a proper reception desk at the entrance. I was feeling like a tourist again and was pleasantly surprised to find that our room was not just a concrete cell, such as I had had in Vietnam, but was en suite with a TV! Susannah and I unpacked as we would be staying in Mandalay for a few days, and we had some supper. I was very careful to talk about being a teacher in England to the friendly staff. We had to be so cautious about anything we said because we didn't know if any of the staff were Christians. We made a point of not mentioning church at all.

On Thursday morning Susannah and I took a taxi to the church we were training at. Justin and Anna made their own way there so that no one would think we were together. The church was situated in a wide avenue and bordered by a brown fence. There were trees in the compound and altogether it was a beautiful place. The training went well and at the end of the day, as we were waiting for our taxi to arrive, I noticed Susannah talking quietly to Justin and Anna. The couple had their luggage with them as they were not returning to the hotel, but staying with some of Anna's relatives in Mandalay. I wondered why Susannah had so much to say to them now, when we'd been with them all day. I was too tired to hear what she was saying and hoped she would finish her conversation soon. At last she finished and we waved goodbye to our interpreters.

Our taxi that evening was a pick-up truck with a covering over the back of it. Susannah and I climbed in the back and we set off. Once again I considered the impracticalities of being tall and larger than the small boned, slim natives. The covering over the back of the truck was so low that I had to bend double. I caught glimpses of Mandalay through the opening in the tarpaulin and hoped the journey wouldn't last too long as I was extremely uncomfortable. Near the church I noticed a run down building and some rickshaws nearby. Glimpses of Mandalay were confused and disjointed as I tried to ease my back and neck. For some reason a pile of bricks by the side of the road stayed in my mind. Then we appeared to drive round a block, nearly in a circle before we finally turned left into the grounds of our hotel.

Just as we were about to retire to bed I realised that I knew nothing about the arrangements for the following day.

"What time are we leaving for the church tomorrow?" I asked Susannah, smothering a yawn.

"You will be picked up at 8.30 am," she said, "A taxi will take you there."

"What about you?" I asked, a bit surprised.

"I am too tired to train," was her reply. "Anna and Justin said I could have the day off tomorrow." She passed me a scrap of paper with a number written on it. "This is the church's telephone number, in case you need it."

I felt a bit shocked and wondered when Susannah would have told me this if I hadn't asked her first.

Despite my worry, I slept well due to exhaustion and woke in the morning feeling as though I could have had a few hours more. I left Susannah in her bed, trying not to feel envious of her "lie-in" and day off. Before 8.30 I was waiting outside the entrance to the hotel for my taxi. 8.30 came and went and as I was supposed to start training at 9.00 I went inside and asked the male receptionist to call the church's number. The phone the other end just rang and rang; no-one answered it at all.

"Where is it you want to go?" asked the receptionist.

"I'm not sure!" I said feeling really stupid. "I met some people there yesterday and said I'd be back to meet them again today at nine o'clock this morning!"

"We'll get another taxi for you," he told me and dialled another number. "It will be here in two minutes!" the man promised me and I walked outside to wait again.

I could feel myself wilting in the humidity as five minutes passed. Another five minutes crept by and I returned to reception.

"The taxi hasn't turned up," I announced.

"Don't worry," said the male receptionist. "We find transport for you!"

A few minutes later a thirty-seater bus arrived at the hotel. I sighed, wondering how many tourists were going out sight-seeing today.

"Come Miss Cook!" the receptionist said, hurrying up to me, "We take you to where you want to go!"

To my amazement he hurried me aboard the bus and said

something in Burmese to the driver. I couldn't believe that they had organised a bus just to take me to church! The bus slowly made its way to the gates and stopped.

"Where is it you want to go?" asked my male companion.

I thought furiously. I couldn't tell them it was a church! What could I say?

"I'm not sure where," I told the driver. "But if I say left or right, will that do?"

"He not speak English," the receptionist told me. "I speak English very good!"

I could feel panic starting to simmer and rise in my stomach. We had made a left turn into the hotel gates the previous night I recalled, so if the bus turned right, I might be able to direct them to the church.

"Turn right," I instructed, praying silently for God's help.

We drove down busy roads and I didn't recognise a thing. I knew I didn't have a good sense of direction but felt sure that this was the wrong way. After a short while I realised we were heading towards the main part of the city and I knew that was wrong. I was sure the church was situated somewhere on the outskirts of Mandalay.

"Stop!" I told the receptionist. "This is the wrong way!"

The receptionist gave orders to the driver who turned the bus around in the middle of the road and we headed back towards the hotel. I felt quite scared by now and was praying constantly to God for guidance. I felt so helpless because I didn't understand a word of Burmese, I wasn't sure that the receptionist could really understand everything that I said and how did I know that the driver wasn't a spy? I desperately wanted just to say, *Take me to the church I visited yesterday*, but knew if I admitted I was in league with the Christians that I could possibly end up in jail. Ahead of us were the wooden gates that led to the hotel and my heart started to speed up.

"Do you want to stop?" the receptionist asked.

Yes! I thought inwardly. I would go and wake Susannah up and tell her she had to come with me because I didn't know where the church was and her taxi hadn't arrived . . . Just then I felt an inner prompting to ask my guides to drive straight on. I shook my head.

"No, don't stop," I requested. "Just keep driving."

We passed the hotel gates on our left and I felt really baffled, because I still didn't know where to go. Suddenly I noticed a pile of bricks that I had espied from the back of the "taxi" the previous evening. A great surge of hope filled me, dispelling the panic and fear. I kept a good look out, aware of the receptionist watching me. We were passing a rundown building when I noticed the rickshaws and knew that the road we had just passed was the road where the church was.

"Stop!" I ordered and the receptionist barked a command to the driver.

Again the driver swung the bus around in the middle of the road and travelled back to the dilapidated building.

"There!" I said excitedly. "That road there!"

The bus swung awkwardly around the corner and travelled slowly along. Ahead I could see the trees in the church complex coming closer. I didn't want the bus to stop right outside the church so I asked to be set down a couple of minutes walk from the complex. Filled with exhilaration I thanked the driver and receptionist and watched them drive away. Once I was sure the bus was far enough away, I walked past the brown fence and entered through the brown gate. I was sure that at least an hour had passed and that I was terribly late. But when I checked my watch as I walked into the church building, I discovered I was only five minutes behind schedule!

Anna and Justin had waited for me to arrive before they began the training session and were very sympathetic about my travels across Mandalay. The forty-two students were eager to learn more that day and they appreciated my way of training. They were not used to having children join in their meetings and neither were they used to actively participating in training. Usually they just sat and listened. But I made them take part in the games and activities and you could see they enjoyed it!

SAGAING

Know therefore that the Lord your God is God; he is the faithful God. (Deuteronomy 7:9)

On Saturday Susannah felt well enough to train again and we took a taxi to and from the church without any problems. On Sunday we met up with Justin and Anna and travelled by taxi to a Sagaing church early in the morning. There were the usual passport checks leaving Mandalay and again when we reached Sagaing. By this time I was getting fed up of having to prove my identity!

Sagaing was located to the west of Mandalay and I was to give a testimony during the service, whilst Susannah was to preach. I felt fairly relaxed about the morning. After all, giving a testimony would take hardly any time as opposed to train-ing all day! Susannah, however, was very tense and hardly spoke a word during our journey to the church. Our taxi was a covered jeep and slightly more comfortable than the pick-up trucks we had travelled in when we'd first arrived in Mandalay.

The church was built in a compound and had trees at its entrance. It had been built in 1888 and miraculously had not been knocked down or used for an alternative purpose.

"Are you coming sightseeing?" I asked Susannah.

She shook her head. "No I have to prepare for my preach-ing later this morning," she said tightly.

"You don't mind if we go?" I said thinking she looked a bit tired again.

"No, that's fine. I need to concentrate."

"OK. We'll see you later."

Leaving Susannah at the church, I spent the morning with Anna and Justin seeing all the official tourist sites in Sagaing including a Buddhist temple built high up in the hills. The view from the temple was amazing. Numerous golden spires rivalled the spire behind me and the sunlight gleamed off the pure white domes and towers of the temples below. White and gold rose at random through the dense tropical trees that spread down to the water's edge. The river was wide and grey and across it ran a metal bridge. On the far side of the river the trees concealed roads and houses, only the temple roofs burst through the dark green leafed canopy. Away in the distance the forest merged with the hills again and the horizon was indistinct, becoming grey and misty. I also visited a hospital and wished that Susannah could have come with me. We had spent very little time relaxing together and I felt I hadn't really got to know her.

The three of us returned to the church and as always, I had to ask to use the facilities, which turned out to be very good! The building was packed and the heat intense. The worship was exuberant yet somehow formal. I gave my testimony during the worship, speaking about God's faithfulness over the years. Anna and Justin took it in turns to interpret both myself and Susannah when she got up to preach. She spoke about the story of Ruth and Naomi and as part of her preaching, Susannah gave her testimony.

"I am from a high caste Indian family," she told us. "My family are very wealthy and we have always had servants. When I am at home I do not have to do anything because the servants see to all the cleaning, washing and cooking. I have worked as a headmistress at a successful Christian school and until I re-trained for children's work, I never had to do anything to dirty my hands. I really thought I was a proper Christian and accepted the status of my family as being normal."

I began to feel slightly uncomfortable, wondering why she was emphasizing her high status.

" When I re-trained, I was sent to the United States to learn how to run children's work in the church. I couldn't believe what I was asked, no, *told* to do. As part of the training we all had to help out with cooking and cleaning which I found hard as I had no experience. But the worst thing of all was having to the clean the toilets. To me that was an insult of the worst kind – that kind of work was for the untouchables!"

I cringed inside at what I considered pomposity. To me, cleaning the toilets was a normal thing to do, I'd been brought up to clean and look after myself. I dreaded what she was going to say next.

"That's when my faith was challenged and I realised I hadn't known the full extent of God's grace in my life. He gave me the grace to do the work of the untouchables."

I was appalled! How could she say such a thing?!

"God's grace crosses cultural barriers," Susannah continued. "If He can enable me to clean toilets think what else, by His grace, He is able to achieve."

I looked around, feeling uncomfortable. To my surprise, the people nearby didn't seem to be offended as I was at her words. They were listening intently to Susannah, drinking in every word. I realised then that although her testimony was offensive to me and my culture, she was speaking straight to the hearts of these people. Looking at it from the caste system perspective, Susannah's story was amazing, showing clearly how God's grace could change a person's life. I was the one out of step and out of line. Feeling humbled, I listened with respect to the rest of her talk.

On our way back to the hotel, Susannah was a lot more

relaxed and quite chatty to begin with. Meantime my camera was busy for there were so many things to take photos of – temples, houses, trees and all the happy looking people we passed. Many people carried umbrellas to keep the sun's heat off and nearly everyone wore a wide, brimmed hat.

I noticed Susannah's energy begin to flag again and as we were nearing the hotel, I asked the driver to stop for another photo. Abruptly she turned to me.

"This will be the last photo!" she said firmly.

Surprised, I agreed, noticing she looked a bit fed up. Well, I thought to myself, she's had to preach and she had obviously been quite nervous about it, so she's probably used up a lot of energy.

Back at the hotel we had supper and I tried to get Susannah to relax and open up a little more. To try and get her talking, I commented on the meal she had ordered.

"Ugh!" I said, trying to be funny. "What's that?" The dish looked like something a cat had brought up.

She stopped eating.

"It is very rude, Monica, to comment on another person's meal," she said sternly.

I apologised and confined my comments to innocuous subjects.

In the morning we packed our bags and paid our bills. I examined my bill carefully, wondering how much the thirty-seater bus was going to cost. To my surprise, all that was listed was my food and bed. They did not charge me for the bus at all!

Susannah and I said goodbye to Anna and Justin and flew from Mandalay to Yangon. There we went our separate ways. Susannah disappeared and I had no idea where she was going. I just had to trust God that she was going to be all right. From Yangon I flew to Bangkok and from there I took a flight to Heathrow. I had plenty of time to ponder the differences in Christians all over the world and how God was using each one of us in very different ways. I was also looking forward to moving around freely in England, without having my passport checked every time I went in or out of a town. There was also the freedom of speech I wanted to enjoy again. I had been so careful all the time I was in Myanmar. Most of all, however, I knew my faith had been tested and strengthened and knew in a deeper way the faithfulness of the God I believed in.

Indian Spring

INDIAN SPRING

I will also make you a light for the Gentiles, that you may bring my salvation to the ends of the earth. (Isaiah 49:6)

I have visited many different countries but no matter where I go in the future, India will always stay with me. It is a land of great beauty and devastating poverty. The heat is a burden you carry with you every day and the dust penetrates every layer of clothing. Travelling is hazardous, the train journeys long and the smells are rank. The people are generous and their wide, joyful smiles accompany you wherever you go. Spectacular, razor sharp mountains contrast with wide-open plains full of sugar cane fields. Eucalyptus trees, banana and coconut palms grow in abundance. In the cities it is all noise and confusion with horns blaring constantly. Sanitation ranges from a shower improvised with a bucket of cold water and a jug, to no facilities at all. Drinking coconut milk and eating off banana leaves with my hands became the norm in the two weeks I spent in this strange land.

Indian Village Evangelism began in August 1983 after one John Timms, from Australia, visited India. What struck John was the poverty endured by millions in southern India and how none of them had ever heard the gospel. Indian Village Evangelism started off in Orakkadu and initially opened a home for both boys and girls. Nowadays the home just houses boys. When we visited Orakkadu there were currently 140 boys in residence. The children in each home are either orphans or from very poor families and each one is sponsored by a Christian in Western Australia. It costs about thirty Australian dollar, (about £12) a month to support one child.

Indian Village Evangelism is currently providing resources for 420 children across their three homes in India. As well as the orphanage in Orakkadu Indian Village Evangelism also has centres at Pannankullan in the South near Tirunelvali as well as a girls' home in the region of Andhra Pradesh which is a region situated to the north west of Madras.

In India the doors are firmly closed to foreign missionaries and only the Indians are free to take the Gospel to their own people. And really, they are the best people to do it. They understand the different customs and cultures, they speak the language and are not viewed with suspicion as foreigners are. The whole Indian Village Evangelism strategy is to enable the Indians to spread the Gospel with Australian support. The Indians need the training and help and once they have been trained they can just get on with putting the teaching into practice.

ORAKKADU

We have become orphans and fatherless. (Lamentations 5:3)

I arrived at Madras Airport at 8.30 pm on Sunday, 11th January 2004 and was overwhelmed by the heat, noise and stench of hot human bodies. The airport swarmed with humanity, many people touting for business and shouting loudly to attract attention. Watching people pass me by I noticed that whole families appeared to be welcoming just one person. Getting used to the heat, noise and smell I looked around for somewhere to sit down and discovered there were no seats. Oh well, I thought, I've been sitting down long enough on a plane. But the heat was wearing and I was feeling extremely tired after the long flight from England. Looking around for boards announcing arrivals, I was accosted by a group of Indians.

"Monica Cook?" asked one of the men. "I am Paul from Orakkadu."

I had forgotten that I was to be met by some of the people from the orphanage. Introductions were quickly made – even our driver was there – and I felt like a giant. The Indians were small and short and I felt as though I was towering over them.

"What time are the Australians arriving?" I enquired of Paul.

"10.30 pm," was his reply.

Hmm, I thought to myself, two hours standing around in this crowd and heat! Talking was difficult because of the noise and I had to lean down and ask the Indians to repeat themselves. 10.30 came and went and even though it should have been cool outside, the heat remained inside the airport. Eleven o'clock approached when Paul spoke again.

"Sorry?" I asked automatically.

"You will recognise the leader from Perth," he shouted. "The man is a giant!"

I chuckled, thinking that everyone who was six foot must seem like a giant to them. A tall man walked through the barrier as another aeroplane discharged its passengers.

"Is that him?" I asked, pointing.

Paul craned his neck, then shook his head. "Not tall enough."

"What about him?" I asked as a skinny man loped into the waiting area.

"Too small," Paul commented.

I really thought Paul was having me on as tall person after tall person was dismissed. When the Australians finally arrived, well after 11.00 pm there was no mistaking their leader.

"Is that him?" I asked as a large, seven-foot tall man strode through the barrier in front of a cluster of travellers.

Paul's face broke into a grin and he started jumping up and down and waving to attract the man's attention. "Alan!" he shouted. "Over here!"

The crowds melted away before Alan as he led the six other Australians to our group.

"I thought there were meant to be eight Australians altogether," I remarked to Paul.

"One of the ladies is here already at the orphanage," he replied.

Alan was far taller than I was and I actually had to look up at him which was quite novel for me. His hands and feet were huge and even though he appeared formidable, there was a calmness and peace about him. When I got to know him I discovered that he was indeed a gentle giant. The three ladies and three other men with Alan were introduced to us and then Paul said;

"Welcome all of you to India. The Indian Village Evangelism team thank you for accepting our invitation."

The Australians looked exhausted and Paul led us out of the airport to the minibus that belonged to the orphanage. We filled the minibus as all the Indians who had accompanied Paul travelled with us also. Between us we had a lot of luggage and there was only just enough room for everyone. The Australians made me feel very welcome and by the end of the journey I felt as though I was part of their team already. I was still a bit confused about who was who, though Alan Cockram with his height was unmistakable. I was introduced to Phil, another Alan, Pam, who I had met before, Andrew, Graeme and Rani.

We arrived at the children's home in Orakkadu well after midnight feeling tired and met up with Rose who had arrived earlier. We were taken to our lodgings, which consisted of three little cottages in the compound. In the bright moonlight I couldn't tell what colour the cottages were but the path leading to each was bordered by white stones that reflected the silver gleam of the moon. I was assigned a two-roomed cottage with Rani. One room was bare so we left all our luggage there, (I couldn't believe how many suitcases Rani had brought. It looked as though her luggage was as much as the rest of us had brought put together!). The other room had two beds in it. We had electric lights, which seemed very modern out in this remote place. The floors of the cottage were made of concrete and it was cool inside. It was about 2.00 am when we put the light out and fell asleep.

I woke suddenly, realising I was in a strange place. Outside I could hear the throaty chorus of frogs that had lulled me to sleep not long ago. I turned over, making myself comfortable. The frogs hadn't disturbed me, so what had woken me so sharply? A wail in the distance broke the peace of the night and made my heart thud loudly. Was someone being murdered? Other voices joined the wails and there appeared to be words in the awful sound that filled the night air. I wondered if some festival was going on. I groaned quietly and pulled the blankets up over my head. It felt as though I'd only been asleep for a couple of hours and we had to be up and dressed by 7.00 am.

The rest of the night passed in fitful slumber and I woke in the morning feeling exhausted. I had a cold shower, which brightened me a little and managed to get myself dressed before 7.00 am. As Rani and I left our cottage to join the others at the gate of the compound, I noticed that the three little cottages were painted green. The earth was pale white dust as far as the eye could see and there were trees planted singly and in clumps throughout the compound. Each of the cottages had a thatched roof but I didn't see any spiders at all, only lizards, which abounded in that place. Rani was quite a character and sharing a room with her, I got to know her well. She had been born in Malaysia but her mother had been Indian and she had lived in Perth since her late teens. Although she knew the languages of India she had only visited her mother's homeland once before. She was younger than me, in her mid-forties and had quite an emotional testimony. Rani had lost one of her sons in the sea at Perth when he was only a young boy.

I gathered with the Australians at the gate, trying to remember their names and saw that all the boys had been assembled to welcome us properly. All 140 of them were lined up on either side of the gate in two long lines that stretched right into the centre of the compound. They were dressed in their home uniform, which consisted of white trousers and white shirt, and they held flower petals in their hands. We walked between the two lines and the boys started shouting and singing their welcome to us. As we passed them, they threw the petals over us – it made us feel like royalty! The two lines came to an end at the centre of the compound where there was podium in a sandy area. We were beckoned up on the stage by a chubby man with a round face and moustache, and the boys stood in lines before the podium as if they were in assembly. The stage was made of wooden blocks, and a keyboard and tall drums stood in one corner. Behind the stage rose a screen with a picture of Jesus and mountains and forests, with the words "Come Ye Blessed of the Father". To one side was a blue board welcoming Alan Cockram and the Australians. The chubby man introduced himself as Tim, one of the directors of Indian Village Evangelism. Some of the boys came up on stage and placed garlands of flowers around each of our necks. The smell of the flowers was strong and sweet and they were coloured pinky red and green. Tim gestured that we should sit whilst the boys remained standing and sang songs to us. The music was Indian and very strange to the Western ear. Next some boys came up onto the stage and performed some drama for us. After that we stood up and each visitor said a little bit about themselves. Then the boys sang to us again and at last it was time for breakfast.

I was hungry, despite being very tired. The boys disappeared to have their breakfast and I was led, with the other visitors, to a table placed under a tree in the compound. Breakfast in

"Breakfast"

the open air was a nice idea, I thought, seating myself beside Rani. The food smelt good, and was served up on banana leaves. I stared at the runny goo on my leaf in dismay. There was no cutlery, which wasn't a problem as I'd always eaten meals with my fingers in Obambo, but I'd never eaten anything quite as fluid as this. I inhaled the scent of curry, carefully scooped a small handful up and raised it slowly to my mouth. The Australians were tucking in, enjoying curry for breakfast. It was very good food but I ate slowly, not wanting to spill anything down my dress. I had a limited supply of fresh clothes and didn't want stale curry smell haunting me for the next two weeks.

Although I'd felt quite hungry, I was soon full and when the Australians had cleared their banana leaves, I finished my meal too.

"Are you sure you've eaten enough?" asked Rani anxiously.

"I'm fine!" I reassured her but the others voiced their concern over my lack of appetite. "I'm quite well," I insisted, refraining from telling them I hadn't wanted to drop the food down my front!

We sat around talking for a bit, letting our curried breakfast digest a little. I caught up with Pam, whom I had met once before. She was the co-founder of IVE along with her husband John Timms. I observed the other Australians, feeling as though I knew them well already. Phil came across as being quite serious, whilst the other Alan was an outspoken, rough diamond. Rose spoke quietly and appeared sensitive and gentle. Andrew, the youngest on the team, was quite shy. Graeme came across as organised and sensible whilst Rani was the loudest and full of enthusiasm for everything.

"Would it be possible to come back during their holidays?" I asked Alan Cockram when the conversation turned to the amount of hours the boys spent at school every day. "I don't suppose they have a lot to do when school's finished." I was thinking of English children getting bored.

"It wouldn't be worth coming here in their holidays," Alan told me. "When there's no school the children are sent back to the village they originally came from. Even if their parents are dead, someone will look after them."

"Why's that?" I enquired.

"The village is where you belong," came the reply. "You always go back to your roots, you know where you belong."

That was quite similar to Obambo, I reflected. I thought that it was a good thing to keep people knowing their roots and identity. The Australians wanted to buy some sports equipment for the boys and so we were all driven in the minibus back to Madras. There were flowers everywhere, draped all over the flat bottomed carts and adorning the people in the streets. The atmosphere was festive and I saw oxen with gilded horns. I couldn't believe the bright colours that had been painted on the horns – the right one was generally blue and the left one yellow and both were decorated with red dots.

"It is the festival of Makar Sankrati," Alan Cockram informed me.

Makar Sankrati is a Hindu festival celebrating the days lengthening as winter moves into spring. There is a special dish that is eaten called Kichadi which is made from ghee and spices. Hindus bathe in the Ganges and worship the sun at this time as he returns in strength for the summer. It is a time when holy deeds are performed such as fasting and charity. For the Hindus, the sun is knowledge, spiritual light and wisdom as well as representing unity, equality and true selflessness. Makar Sankrati signifies for the Hindus that they should turn away from the darkness of delusion in which they live and begin to joyously let the light within them shine brighter. This festival causes Hindus to reflect on how they can begin to grow in purity, wisdom and knowledge, just as the days begin to lengthen and bring more light into the world.

I found the meaning behind Makar Sankrati interesting and compared it to the Christian message of encouragement we were bringing during the festival. For our team and the Indian Christians, the Son of God was knowledge and spiritual light. We believed that it was the Spirit of God that united us as Christians and brought about a spirit of true selflessness. We also believed that in letting the light of God shine into our lives, we would grow in purity, wisdom and knowledge.

When we returned from buying the sports equipment we discovered the compound full of boys playing and talking.

"Why aren't they all at school?" I asked.

"It is part of the Makar Sankrati festival," replied Alan, who seemed to know everything that was going on. "They get today off school."

So we spent the rest of the day with the boys, getting to know them and sharing out the sports equipment. All the boys wanted to talk to us, to practise their English. The older boys loved the bats and balls and soon organised a cricket match. Others sorted themselves into pairs and played badminton. The younger ones got hold of some of the skipping ropes and took it in turns pretending to be horses and riders.

Usually the day is very structured at the children's home. The boys wake up at 5.00 am and do an hour of homework. At 6.00 am they do their chores, which include sweeping and cleaning the compound with brooms. At 7.00 am they have thirty minutes of Bible study followed by washing, and cleaning their teeth. (On Tuesday morning I woke up and looked out to see the yard full of naked children around the water points in the compound!) Then they change into their school uniforms and have breakfast at 8.00 am. After that they go to school. The primary school is quite close by so the younger ones walk there. The older boys cycle, as the secondary school is further away. They return to the home at around 4.00 pm and have free time until 6.00 pm. During this time they have a drink, play cricket and wash their clothes – although a laundry man does visit regularly. At 6.00 pm they do an hour's homework and at 7.00 pm they have another thirty minutes of Bible study. The evening meal takes place at 8.00 pm and they have to be in bed by nine o'clock.

PANNANKULLAN

But the needy will not be forgotten, nor the hope of the afflicted ever perish. (Psalm 9:18)

We left Orakkadu before the boys returned from school on the Tuesday, taking the minibus to the train station in Madras. We caught a train at 5.00 pm down to the south, to Pannankullan. We took a first class sleeper train as the journey was quite long and we wouldn't be arriving at our destination until morning. The cabins weren't too bad and I shared mine with Rani. They were really just berths with a curtain to draw across for some privacy. Otherwise the berths opened into the communal corridor. Half way through the night, nature called and I found my way to the toilet, which was very basic. I managed to find my way back into the corridor and then realised that all the curtains looked the same in the subdued light. Which curtain concealed my berth? Cautiously I pulled one curtain aside slightly and saw pair of very large feet sticking out from under the blankets. That was definitely not Rani. I tried the next curtain and a chorus of snores hit my ears, which had previously been muffled by the curtain. It sounded as though a troop of men were sleeping in that berth so I let the curtain fall back in place. Holding my breath I lifted the edge of the next curtain and sighed with relief. It was my cabin and I slipped into bed without waking Rani in the berth next to me. In the morning Rani heard my adventure with roars of laughter. We were both so very different but got on incredibly well.

We arrived at Pannankullan at 5.00 am on Wednesday. All of us were blinking like day-struck owls, having been woken only half an hour previously. We stared around at the station as the train rumbled off, continuing its journey south. We appeared to be in the middle of nowhere. Indeed, the only sign that we'd arrived somewhere was a board with the name of the station written on it, and that was it. We were in the middle of the countryside with not a house in sight! We waited for a while and eventually a minibus from the orphanage arrived and we were driven to our destination. The journey took between thirty and forty-five minutes and our arrival at Pannankullan children's home was very similar to our welcome at Orakkadu. At the gate and inside the compound were white chalk patterns beneath WELCOME TO OUR GUESTS written in coloured chalk. Coloured chalk drawn flowers decorated the ground around us and the word welcome was also written twice so that the two words bisected each other.

"Welcome"

In the right angles, pretty coloured butterflies had been sketched. The girls welcoming us wore white blouses and dark blue skirts.

The girls' day was structured in a similar fashion to the boys' routine at Orakkadu, except that at 4.00 pm they had a shower and washed their uniforms, and then they were free. We took skipping ropes, bangles and beads to give to for the girls in the home, which they were delighted with.

We spent Wednesday and Thursday in Pannankullan and saw how different the country was. In Pannankullan the soil was quite red, (though a different shade to Obambo), and there were more palm trees growing there. The land was tilled, everywhere we went we saw plough marks in the red earth. Down in the south the land was green and lush. The hills were forested and the sky a perfect blue. (We had no rain at all during the two weeks we spent in India.) The heat was intense and the sun shone fiercely down on us every day. I found the temperature very pleasant as it was winter back home in England. The

Australians however, found the weather quite chilly as they'd come from the heat of their summer. Flowers blossomed everywhere and the fields were cultivated. The main roads were good but the little tracks that took us to remote places were horrendous. Wide flat plains contrasted with massive mountains. Down in the south there were a lot of oxen and carts and here the oxen had both their horns painted red. The typical scene was of the fields being cultivated either by hand tools or by oxen. Whilst at the home in Pannankullan we heard of several nasty accidents involving cars colliding with oxen carts.

During the daylight hours we visited many different workshops that had been set up as a cover for church activities. We saw a tailoring school and a crèche for children, so that their mothers could go out to work. There was also a typing school with very high standards. At each place we visited we either prayed or sang some worship songs as part of a workshop, even though most of the workshop candidates were Hindu! We also encouraged the Indian Christians in the work that they were doing.

On the Wednesday evening the girls put on a concert for us. Afterwards I was asked to speak and taught the orphans how precious each one of them was in the eyes of God. It was a relief to spend some time encouraging Christians, rather than teaching or training them; though the numerous visits we made to all their projects were exhausting in a different way! We ate both days at the home, the dishes being mainly curried meat and vegetables.

On the Thursday, before we returned to Orakkadu, we all planted a tree at the children's home. Each visitor took it in turns to place a young sapling in the soil and planted it gently in the ground. When it was my turn I lifted the sapling up and prayed for the girls and their situations before placing it in the earth. I think the saplings may have been eucalyptus – they were thin plants with large, rounded leaves. Afterwards I discovered that each tree would have a plaque fixed to it with the name of the planter engraved upon it. I thought that was a bit over the top but it was the Indians' way of expressing their thanks for our support. In the evening we took a sleeper train back to Madras and all slept soundly, tired out from all the places we'd visited.

ANDHRA PRADESH

But blessed is he who is kind to the needy. (Proverbs 14:21b)

On the Friday we had a bit of a rest at the Orakkadu orphanage and discussed what we had seen so far. I felt as though I was getting to know the Australians better and they included me in everything they did. Alan Nicol teased young Andrew about the attention the girls at Pannankullan had given him, asking him if he was thinking of taking an Indian wife! Phil and Rose diverted the conversation and started talking about cricket which Andrew loved. Although Rose was quiet she was a deeply caring person and Phil, who was quite serious, was also very emotional. Pam, Alan the Gentle Giant and Graeme discussed our next trip to Andhra Pradesh. Rani waxed lyrical about everything we had seen so far and wanted to know when we were going shopping so she could practise her bartering skills and the Indian language.

It was early in the morning on Saturday when we left by minibus for the orphanage in the region of Andhra Pradesh. Our driver was a man employed by the orphanage, called Silas. The little breakfast I'd managed to swallow before leaving, was threatening to come up as we were shaken around on the rough roads. Later, when the sun had risen, the road became quite hazardous. Our driver was very sensible but we were constantly at risk from the other drivers on the road. Ox drawn carts were easy to avoid but other cars just raced along the middle of the road expecting everyone else to get out of their way. After four hours of this kind of travelling we were all exhausted and quite shaky, and relieved to have arrived at the orphanage. One of the first things I noticed were the oxen passing by, either taking their owners and cart to the nearest town or heading out to the fields. Without a single exception the oxen had both horns painted red.

Again we were welcomed in the traditional Indian fashion but this time the garlands of flowers consisted of greenery and pinky red blooms with bright yellow flowers at either end. The orphanage was for girls only and they made us feel like royalty again. After we had been welcomed we introduced ourselves and told our testimonies to the girls. Rani's story was still the most moving, even though we'd heard it several times already. Then we were shown around the school as the girls went to their lessons. The orphanage here was fairly large and they had built a primary school on the site so the youngest girls didn't have to walk far to school during the week. We learnt that the leaders of the place had plans to build an English medium school on the site as well. This kind of school would equate to an English secondary school but I was unsure about the wisdom in such a plan. I had liked what I had seen at the boys' orphanage where the boys were given a home and place to grow up but at the same time they were already living in the world by having to go out to school. I wondered if having both schools on site would protect the girls too much and not prepare them enough for the outside world when they had to find a job. I was impressed with the standard of education at the primary school though and learnt that the teachers also provide typing lessons for the girls. The teachers were all highly qualified and set very high standards for their pupils.

We ate at the home and had curry for lunch – by now we were all getting used to eating with our fingers. Afterwards we rested. We had been given two rooms, one for the women and the other for the men. The women's room was quite small and our four beds were squeezed into a tiny area. The beds were actually touching each other and there was a mosquito net on each bed. We decided to lie down and rest as the heat was intense and we felt pretty tired from all the travelling the night before. As soon as I lay down, my eyes felt heavy and I drifted off to sleep quite quickly. I woke with a start, hearing women's voices around me.

"Too late!" chuckled Rose. "She's awake now!"

I rubbed my eyes and sat up, feeling bleary. The other three women were sitting on their beds, clutching their pillows.

"Hello!" I said. "Did you have a good rest? I think I fell asleep!"

"You did!" laughed Rani. "And you snored dreadfully. We couldn't get to sleep at all!"

"We were very tempted to throw pillows at you, to stop you snoring," smiled Pam.

I apologised for my antisocial behaviour and we spruced ourselves up. Meeting up with the men, we spent some time with the girls, teaching and encouraging them. When we had finished, the girls put on a concert for us and we crowded into a small hall. The girls danced and sang for us on a raised stage at one end of the hall and we applauded and cheered their efforts. Their costumes were bright and their performances loud and energetic. During the concert we taught them a couple of songs and at the end I was invited to speak. Using visual aids I spoke about God's love for each one of them.

After the concert, the orphans showed us around their home. The girls were all very pretty and their laughter rang in the air as they played and took us to various places in the orphanage compound. They enjoyed having some individual attention and each of our team was "adopted" by a small group. I noticed that there were a lot of girls vying for shy Andrew's attention. One group took me to their favourite place – a swing. They let me have a go on their swing – though I was a little worried I'd break it. It didn't look too strong and all the girls were small and slim. I just sat on the swing and was relieved that it didn't collapse.

We watched the sun set beyond the distant mountains with our new friends and then went back to the home to eat. We were also offered drinks and at first I didn't realise that what I was being offered was a drink. I held the large, round, green fruit in both hands and watched the others sideways to see what they were doing. One of the girls handed me a straw and I noticed a hole had been cut into the top of the fruit. Carefully I stuck the straw in the hole and took a cautious sip, realising that this was a drink, not a snack. The taste was creamy and well, different.

"Do you like coconut milk?" one of the orphans asked me.

I nodded vigorously and drank some more. It was an odd taste but quite refreshing. I hesitated to call it milk though because it was nothing like milk back in England!

After we'd eaten we rested before going to bed. Apparently I didn't snore during the night. On Sunday morning we took the church service for the girls and spent some more time with them. Shy Andrew looked very embarrassed as the girls continued to demand his attention. After lunch we said goodbye and as we drove off in the minibus the girls waved madly at us. We started driving back to Orakkadu but about halfway between the two orphanages, the driver suddenly turned off the main road down a really rough track to a church building in the middle of nowhere.

This was one of the many churches we officially opened during our trip. The church building was nearly finished and as the church leader already had a congregation of twenty-five members we performed the opening ceremony. We then led the first service to be held in the church. After the service I asked where the nearest toilet was and was informed that there was no toilet. So, armed with my

Children watched as we drove down the rough track

ever-decreasing supply of paper hankies, I retreated into the dense bushes surrounding the church building, experiencing a momentary longing for the public conveniences of England. The bushes had thorns on them that tangled in my clothes. However much I tried to find a space big enough for me, I just kept snagging my dress. In the end I gave up and returned to the minibus. I then had the bouncy journey back to the boys' orphanage to contend with but when we at last reached Orakkadu, I finally found a usable toilet!

CHRISTIANS IN ORAKKADU

. . . they will lay hands on you and persecute you. They will deliver you to synagogues and prisons and you will be brought before kings and governors, and all on account of my name. (Luke 21:12)

On the Monday after we'd returned from Andhra Pradesh we set out again to visit several local churches. Indian Village Evangelism sends hundreds of men and women to Bible college in India in order to provide leaders for the churches that are springing up everywhere. Indian Village Evangelism rely on individuals and churches support to train people and to provide financially for them once they are trained. When I was visiting India it cost Indian Village Evangelism 120 Australian dollars a month to support a male preacher and 40 Australian dollars a month for a female Bible teacher. The male preachers concentrate on preaching, prayer and pastoring. They visit the sick occasionally as well. The female Bible teachers support the preachers by visiting the sick and running children's meetings. There are very few Bibles available to the churches and only a few people can read. So much of the teaching in the churches is done by means of stories and song. The leaders write songs, which include doctrine so that their congregations can memorise Bible teaching easily. Each pastor has to have a minimum of twenty-five members in his church before finances are released to erect a church building.

All this is happening in a climate of repression and persecution. The population in India numbers around a hundred million and eighty per cent of the nation is Hindu. In 2004 the government was being run by a Hindu party and Christians were forbidden to buy land to build churches on, baptise converts or convert Hindus to Christianity. So Indian Village Evangelism were operating under the shield of Community Support – opening orphanages and church buildings disguised as tailor shops, childcare centres and training centres for office skills. These community projects were supported by the government as long as the Christians didn't hold meetings outside of the church buildings. The churches provided workshops to train ordinary people in practical skills so they could find a better job and improve their standard of living. Many of the people attending these workshops were Hindus so the workshops were really outreach meetings! Every day the churches held a Christian service before the workshop started and always ended the workshop with prayer. The delegates are always made aware of this but still come along and by the end of the course, most of the Hindus become Christians!

In the more remote villages the pastors and their families are often persecuted, not by the authorities, but by the people they are trying to help. They often have to escape from the village they have been working in and sometimes they lose their lives. The villagers sometimes whip and beat them up and many times leave the Christians for dead. If they manage to escape they will set up home somewhere else and try again. I was impressed by their tenacity. The Christians will not give up. "How long will it be before the door is completely closed?" they ask. "That's why we do the work we can do now."

I met two brothers – Paul and Timothy – who were directors of the work Indian Village Evangelism support in the Orakkadu region. They both wrote many of the songs that were used in the local churches. Timothy lived near the orphanage at Orakkadu and struggled with ongoing illness including asthma. His brother Paul lived further away but they both were responsible for the pastors and Christian workers in the region. They had ingenious ways of meeting with the people they looked after so as not to attract unwanted attention. One week they would meet up with some of their people at a prayer and fasting session. The next week it might be a meeting for some teaching elsewhere with a different group of people. Also, once a month the leaders of each church in the region meet up at a different church. When they meet at one particular church they spend the day worshipping, receiving teaching and also support that church in whatever way it needs supporting. For instance, if that church has a lot of sick people the leaders from all the other churches will go out and visit all the sick in one afternoon. Or if the children's work is struggling the leaders will organise a children's meeting to be held that day and provide teaching, training and games. The whole set-up is quite fluid and flexible and will provide whatever support is needed at any one time.

We travelled far on that Monday and visited a fair number of churches. At each church we'd eat a meal after the service was over. We'd all sit on the floor and eat off banana leaves. I was reminded of Kenya as hospitality in India is as important as it is in Obambo. The churches provided more than enough food at each meal. Even though the cooking was done over open fires in quite primitive conditions the results were excellent! The toilets were few and far between however and in the last village we visited there were no toilets at all and I was beginning to run low on paper hankies. This village had provided us with an amazing welcome. At the entrance to the church was "Heartly Welcome" in chalk and surrounded by chalk drawn flowers. The church was Rimes Church of Christ Basthapalayam – but I never did find out what the name meant!

On the way back to Orakkadu we saw a lovely sight. The road ran over a bridge which spanned a narrow river and the driver stopped the minibus when I asked him to. There was a herd of buffaloes swimming across the water. They were a great, heaving mass of dark, wet flanks, ploughing through the blue water, making it foam. As we watched and took photos, the leading animals gained the far side and hauled themselves awkwardly up out of the water, hooves churning the earth bank to mud. The sunlight gleamed off wet skin and curved horns and the whole herd appeared to move as one.

LOST IN RED HILL

Your word is a lamp to my feet and light for my path. (Psalm 119:105)

On Tuesday we visited an area called Red Hill in Orakkadu to do the "tourist" bit and to look around a little. Red Hill was a shopping area and frequented by both tourists and local people. Crowds dressed in bright colours thronged the narrow roads. As we drove through the streets it seemed as though all the men were handsome and all the women beautiful. Brightly coloured clothes fluttered everywhere – red, orange, green and yellow with golden thread and shiny embroidery flashing in the sunlight. Baggy trousers in vibrant hues set off the loose white tops the men wore. The women's saris were decorated and tiny gold or silver coloured sandals showed beneath the hems of their long dresses. It was a riot of colour that should have clashed, but somehow made a harmonious whole.

Silas parked the minibus from the orphanage at the side of a main road and we wandered out into the hot, smelly street. The noise was incredible, shouting, laughing, talking, hawking. The shops were tiny and profuse and there seemed to be everything one could want in a single road. The scene reminded me of 1950s type shops. There were hardware stores, material shops, dress making enterprises, food stores and kitchenware shops. Everyone wanted to have a set of genuine Indian clothes so the plan was that we would buy our material in one shop and then go to another shop to have the clothes made up. Crowding into one of the tiny shops we looked at the variety of materials available. Unsurprisingly, the men all made up their minds pretty quickly as to what cloth they liked.

"How much do you think Alan will need to buy?" Alan Nicol asked Rani. "There's a lot of him!"

Alan the Gentle Giant laughed and cuffed him round the ear. Alan Nicol ducked and backed into shy Andrew.

"Hey Andrew!" Alan Nicol looked at the material Andrew had chosen. "You'll look stunning in that! All those girls at the orphanages will definitely want to be your wife!"

Andrew blushed and looked at the floor.

"Come on Alan," Phil said seriously. "You need to decide on your cloth too."

"Rani, will you help us barter?" asked Graeme.

Rani took over the purchasing and after paying, the men announced that they were ready.

I hadn't even chosen which pattern or colour I wanted and none of the other women were ready to move on either. So it was decided by the men that they would take the minibus up to the next shop and start getting their suits made up. Once they'd gone, some of the other women started making plans as to which shops they'd visit on the walk along the road to meet the men. I was quite leisurely about choosing my material but eventually decided on some navy cloth with a gold motif embroidered on it. Having purchased my material with Rani's help, I said I'd start walking slowly because of my hip and set off. Rani decided to stay and help the other women barter for their goods. I had no idea how far along the other shop was but thought I'd be able to recognise it if I saw the orphanage minibus near it.

As I walked along, enjoying the hustle and bustle and general atmosphere, I discovered that there were quite a few minibuses around and that they all looked identical to the one from the orphanage. Wandering up the road in Red Hill I soon discovered that not everyone dressed nicely. Out of a side alley two beggars in rags and stinking of filth lunged at me. Part of me did want to help them but we had been warned at the orphanage of beggars who would rob you. So I stared ahead ignoring their cries and walked on. And on, and on and on. Until I suddenly realised I had no idea where I was.

Shops stretched in every direction and the roads and pavements were still filled with brightly dressed people. I stopped and turned around but couldn't work out which street I had just come out of – they all looked so similar. Something cold and heavy squirmed in my stomach and I felt panic rising. I didn't speak the language, had no idea where I was and was worried about meeting more beggars.

"Lord," I prayed silently. "Help! I've no idea where I am!"

One street appeared slightly more familiar than the others so I re-traced my steps although my legs felt really wobbly. I reckoned I'd walked about two miles altogether from the material shop and walked another mile before I stopped again. The area around me looked vaguely familiar but I still had no idea where I was. Out of the roaring traffic drove a motorbike, which came to a halt beside me. The driver grinned and I recognised Silas. I gaped at him, wondering how he had found me.

"Come on!" he said. "I'll take you back to the others."

Mystified as to why he was now driving a motorbike, I got on behind him feeling very undignified. I was wearing a dress which was now rucked up above my knees. Clutching my bag with one hand I held onto the driver's belt with my other hand. Silas revved the bike up and we were away. It was Vietnam all over again and this time I had no mask or hat. Weaving in and out of the traffic I felt exceedingly unsafe and flung both arms around Silas. There appeared to be no traffic rules at all but somehow we made it back to the minibus unscathed. Poor Silas was red in the face by the time he dismounted. I think I'd wrapped my arms around him too hard. Everyone cheered as I got off the motorbike – everyone including the crowd around us! Silas was laughing.

"We saw you!" said Alan the Giant.

"We were sitting at the back of the minibus," said Graeme.

"We'd got our suits organised and had come back here, waiting for everyone and we saw you walk past on the other side of the road!" Alan laughed.

"You looked like you knew where you were going!" smiled Graeme. "And we couldn't see that you'd walked right past the shop because there was another minibus blocking our view."

"We did think of sending Andrew out to look for you," said Alan Nicol. "But thought he might get abducted by the Indian girls around."

Andrew blushed again but he was laughing.

"So how did you find me?" I asked.

"By the time we got to the dressmaker's shop," said Pam, "The men had realised you were missing."

"So I borrowed someone's motorbike," said Silas, "And just drove off up the road and there you were!"

I looked around and saw an alleyway opposite the minibus.

"I got approached by some very vocal beggars," I told them, pointing across the road. "I was looking straight ahead then and wouldn't have seen anything!"

Rani took me to the dressmaker's shop to put in my order for my baggy trousers and dress and was told we could collect all our orders in two days' time. Later that afternoon when we were back at the orphanage, the boys insisted we play cricket with them. Not being terribly keen on cricket and having no idea how it is played, I declined and sat at the sidelines watching. The Australians played hard and the Indian boys did really well. At one point, however, someone missed a catch and as I was drifting a little, feeling a bit tired, I didn't realise what was happening and failed to move out of the way. The ball struck the ground close by and then hit my lower leg. I bit my lip, blinking back the tears. I'd just discovered another reason for not being interested in cricket. The game was stopped for a while until they ascertained I was all right. My leg really did hurt and a bruise developed quite quickly, making the skin sore for several days. The game of cricket was declared a draw as it was nearly time for the boys to do their homework and the Australians handed out a collection of hats and caps to the boys that had been contributed by some Australian churches.

IRRAKUM ISLAND

Therefore in the east give glory to the Lord; exalt the name of the Lord, the God of Israel, in the islands of the sea. (Isaiah 24:15)

Indian Village Evangelism has a church they support on Irrakum Island which is a tiny place, just off the coast of Madras. On Wednesday we were due to visit the church and meet the congregation so we set off early in the morning. Silas dropped us off from the minibus on the coast in the middle of nowhere with sand underfoot and the sea to the east. The edge of the sea was a long way off but apparently the minibus could go no further due to the mud. Timothy was with us and led the way towards the sea, keeping a look out for the boat he'd arranged to take us to the island.

We set out, tramping our way through wet sand and mud. I was wearing a dress and stout sandals and could feel the wet sand spattering up my legs and along the hem of my dress. After a short while my calves began to ache. I was quite used to standing for long periods of time or walking around on concrete or hard earth, but moist sand and clinging mud were exhausting to travel through. Ahead of us the sea sparkled in the sunlight and heat poured over us. There was hardly any wind. In the sea bobbed many boats, large and small, mostly made from wood.

At length we reached the edge of the sea and Timothy found the boat that was to take us to the island. It turned out that the boat owners were friends of Indian Village Evangelism and had agreed to lend us their boat for the day, but they were manning it. As the Australians clambered aboard I looked out to sea and saw a dark silhouette of an island miles and miles away. There were no other islands nearby and I realised that the isle on the horizon must be Irrakum. My heart sank at the thought of being such a long time on the water. Due to my hip replacement I found it difficult to get on board and had to be helped by Alan the Giant and Graeme. I felt like a beached whale rolling over the side of the boat and clumsily staggered to where the women were sitting.

Once aboard I sat very still whilst the Australians relaxed and chatted amongst themselves, taking photos of each other and of me! I sat in the front of the boat and watched the shoreline slowly recede. To begin with the boat was punted across the water. Timothy explained that the water was very shallow for quite a way out so punting was the only way to move along. Also, as there was no breeze we had no help from the sails so close to land. I held onto my seat tightly, feeling splinters digging into my palms. Waiting for the inevitable sea-sickness to start I let my eyes wander around my surroundings.

The boat was crudely made with no finishing off that I'd seen on the other boats around. It looked as though roughly cut logs had just been lashed tightly together with ropes that had seen better days. My eyes moved upwards to the rope rigging and the limp tarpaulin sails swinging idly in the calm air. Around me came sounds of laughter and conversation as the Australians tactfully left me alone. Graeme and Phil were talking about how the Indians' need for more teaching could be met. Alan the Giant was talking and laughing with Timothy. Alan Nicol was teasing Andrew about how many hearts he was going to break today. Rani was unusually quiet, gazing out over the sea as Pam and Rose talked softly. The water lapped spasmodically around the boat as the owner punted his vessel through the sea. The air smelt of salt, fish and sweat. The sun was rising higher and beating down upon us. I could feel my nose beginning to burn and peel but I didn't dare move to get more sun cream out of my bag in case seasickness struck.

After a while a breeze flapped the empty sails against the roughly carved masts and the owner of the boat put his punting pole away. In less than ten minutes we were moving smoothly, gliding this way and that across the water towards the island which appeared only fractionally larger than it had from the shore. I heard the Australians talking about picking up the wind now we were out of the shelter of the shoreline, and they spoke about tacking into the wind. Waiting for the seasickness to engulf me I remained frozen, a fixed smile on my face.

Although the journey took two hours, I did not suffer from seasickness at all. The water was fairly calm, even using the wind to help us on the way there. The boat was run onto the beach at Irrakum Island and I got up stiffly. My joints and muscles ached from the uncomfortable seat and from being immobile for such a long time. Timothy and Alan the Giant helped me down onto the sand and I walked slowly up the beach. The boat owner stayed with his vessel I noticed as I looked back. The white sand ceased abruptly at the top of the rise and dense greenery took over. Low trees and bushes surged across the landscape and we followed a path to a small village. The houses were made of wood and had thatched roofs. In the shade of nearby trees several Nubian type goats were resting, opening their dark, hard eyes to stare disinterestedly at us.

The church on Irrakum was made of concrete and held their congregation of between forty and fifty people quite easily. We all took part in a two hour long service and afterwards shared a curried lunch with the congregation. Although the atmosphere was pleasant I found it a bit odd that the church just seemed to want money from us, not teaching. I never got a chance to ask Timothy how long Indian Village Evangelism had been supporting them and wondered if they were cut off from the persecutions that were troubling the churches on the mainland.

After we'd finished lunch Rose asked for the toilet. I was close by and heard someone tell her there was no toilet at the church but that some of the Irrakum women would take her to a place she could use as a toilet. Less than five minutes later she was back with the four women who'd accompanied her. I was wondering if I should ask for the toilet as well but when I saw her shocked face, I thought I'd better ask her what it was like.

"Don't go," she whispered, "Unless you're really desperate."

"Why?" I asked. "Is it that bad?"

"Well," she looked around to make sure no-one was too near to hear, "There really isn't a toilet. They take you to a circle of bushes and then just stand around and watch you go!"

I comforted Rose and decided I wasn't desperate. With the hot sun producing lots of sweat and having had very little to drink, I decided I could wait until we returned to the orphanage. Next however, we walked on to another village where we taught and encouraged the Christians there. They offered us yet another curry before we went.

On our walk back through the shrubs and trees to the beach, we passed several large, still ponds. At the edge of one of them stood a tall, white heron, a striking pose against the dark background. On coming out of the trees to the sandy beach we noticed the change in the weather immediately. It was still hot but sand swirled into our eyes as we hurried down to the boat. The wind was so strong by now that all the owner had to do was push off, raise the sails and steer as the wind blew us straight back to the mainland. In contrast to the outward journey, our return trip only lasted half an hour!

MADRAS

When the Gentiles heard this, they were glad and honoured the word of the Lord; and all who were appointed for eternal life believed. (Acts 11:48)

I woke on Thursday morning with a tickly throat and congestion in my nose. Trying to ignore my symptoms I joined the Australians as they visited Madras. It was their last day and I wanted to spend as much time with them as possible. The men insisted on visiting the cricket ground and walked all around it whilst us ladies sat in the shade and talked. I noticed that whenever Andrew talked about cricket he lost his painfulness shyness and became animated. Wherever we went that day the Australian men would strike up conversations with Indian men and inevitably the talk would turn to cricket. I suppose it was a good point of conversation but I got pretty fed up of test matches by the end of the day!

In the afternoon we decided to go on a sightseeing tour that Silas offered to take us on. He showed us the coastal sites of Madras but whilst on the outskirts of the city, the minibus broke down. I quite welcomed the rest as I was beginning to cough and I felt as though I had some sort of bronchitis. The driver disappeared to find a telephone and the Australians got off the bus. Despite feeling lousy, I realised that staying on a stuffy bus wasn't going to do my bronchitis any good. So I stood outside in the sun, trying to breathe normally and enjoy the last few hours with my friends.

Silas came dashing back to tell us that a friend of his who had a minibus would come and pick us up and take us back to the orphanage for supper. While we waited for Silas' friend,

Silas started sorting out what was wrong with his bus and we stood around talking. We had been discussing some of the churches we'd visited and had been speaking quite loudly. Suddenly I noticed two policemen approaching us and pointed them out to my friends.

The two men were short and dark, dressed in khaki coloured uniforms which consisted of a short-sleeved shirt and long trousers. The uniform was more western style than Indian and they had radios clipped onto their belts which chattered and hissed. They also wore black caps with a badge on the front. We watched them as they stopped in front of us, looking aggressive. I noticed that Silas had disappeared beneath the minibus.

"Are you Christians?" barked one of the policemen.

We looked at each other in concern. Had they overheard our conversation? We knew we couldn't say that we were Christians because that would be considered evangelism which was illegal. Not wanting to leave too long a silence which might incriminate us I ventured a reply.

"We're tourists."

"That's right," said Alan the Giant amiably. "We're just out for the day."

"We're staying in Orakkadu," volunteered Graeme.

"*We're* Christians," announced the second policeman.

There was a moment of stunned silence and Silas re-appeared from beneath the minibus. We talked for ages with the policemen who were particularly interested in my work in England. I realised that with the policemen around, no-one else was bothering us. I could see vendors and hopefuls hovering a good distance away. One of the policemen asked me to email him when I returned to England so that they'd know I'd got back safely. I took his email address but was a bit uncertain as to his motivation.

Silas' friend Titus appeared in his minibus and we all climbed aboard.

"Tell Paul I'll be back soon!" Silas called. "I've nearly fixed it."

"Can you take us to the airport this evening?" Graeme shouted.

Silas nodded and waved goodbye.

On our way back to the orphanage we stopped off at Red Hill in Orakkadu to pick up our Indian-style suits. Back at the orphanage I couldn't eat much supper as I was coughing so badly. Feeling quite wretched I said goodbye to the Australians as they left once supper was over. Silas was back by then and took them to the airport. I would have liked to have gone with them to the airport to see them off but I had to pack and all my body wanted to do was sleep. Paul brought me some medicine for my cough and then I went to bed.

LEAVING INDIA

For there is no difference between Jew and Gentile – the same Lord is Lord of all and richly blesses all who call on him. (Romans 10:12)

On Friday morning when I awoke, I was amazed to find I felt better! The bronchitis had disappeared over night. I had no idea what the Indians put in their medicine but it definitely worked!

However, once I was at the airport in the stuffy heat and assailed on every side by smells of sweat and different body odours, the congestion in my chest and throat returned. After I had said goodbye to my Indian hosts I had quite a wait and as there was nowhere to sit, I was feeling dizzy. There were people packed wall-to-wall and I felt foggy and confused. Where was I supposed to go? I headed for the security desk to get rid of my luggage and suddenly I found I wasn't pushing through a sea of humanity anymore. I got my luggage booked in very quickly and was thinking that this was going to be easier than I had imagined. I asked where I should go next and was directed to the passport check.

In England and other countries I was used to lining up in an orderly fashion and a lot of places have the lines cordoned off so it is easy to join a queue. Here, at Madras Airport however, there were no queues. There was a sudden surge of people who came up behind and just pushed in front of me. There were four people checking passports who made no effort to organise us into queues. They just looked at the next passport shoved in their face and checked the photo against the person standing in front of them. All the time the heat and humidity were increasing and the nearer I got to the passport check, the more difficult it was to move. Then a boy fainted because of the heat and the smells. That made me really angry. Fortunately he was dragged out of the crowd before he could get crushed but I had had enough of being pushed around.

I tried coughing, which wasn't difficult as the bronchitis was worsening. That had no effect at all, people just turned away. So I stuck my elbows out and when someone pushed me aside, I pushed back. Amazingly, all resistance to my progress ceased and I was allowed to move to the front of the queue. After my passport was checked I had to go to another desk and re-identify my luggage. This, I was told, was due to bomb scares. I watched yet another label being stuck on my suitcases which were then placed on a trolley and I followed them out to the aeroplane, enjoying my personal space once again.

Once we'd taken to the air, I got out my notebook and pencil and reflected on the things I had learnt whilst in India. I had found the Indians' perseverance in the face of adversity a real challenge. The Indian Christians were willing to give their whole lives for the sake of the Gospel. And I had felt such a part of the Australian family, despite being the only English person around. I knew that was part of being a Christian and having an extended family wherever I went, even if I hadn't met the people before.

The aeroplane levelled out and headed away from India leaving behind the heat and the sun, the Hindu festivals and the hard-working Christians. I was on my way home.

The Faces of Kenya

PART ONE – OBAMBO

But you, O God, do see trouble and grief; you consider it to take it in hand. The victim commits himself to you; you are the helper of the fatherless. Break the arm of the wicked and evil man; call him to account for his wickedness that would not be found out. (Psalm 10:14–15)

Tuesday 30th March to Thursday 1st April – Travelling Experiences

Five weeks! I thought to myself as the aeroplane touched down at Nairobi Airport. Five whole weeks of being in Kenya – Obambo, Mombasa and Narok! I smiled to myself, enjoying the knowledge that I wouldn't see England for well over a month. It was Tuesday, 30th March 2004 and I wasn't due to return to England until 5th May.

I was met, as usual by Pastor Jack at the airport, along with his brother Sylvester and Jack's nephew William. We exchanged greetings and Pastor Jack arranged for a taxi to take the four of us and my luggage (I had double checked this time that I'd picked up the right bags) to Sylvester's house. On arriving at the house I was aware that Sylvester's wife was nowhere to be seen. Instead, I recognised Jack's second eldest daughter, Janet, looking after her cousins. Janet smiled and welcomed me, making me feel at home. She seemed to be a regular part of the household and I felt reluctant to ask where Sylvester's wife was. I was afraid of upsetting people, in case she had died.

The following morning as Pastor Jack and I walked through the slums to the main road to catch a bus, I plucked up courage to ask him what had happened to Sylvester's wife. But just as I was about to speak, he started explaining about the new regulations for travelling by bus.

"I don't know if you know," he began, "But we have a new government here in Kenya and they have made many changes. We now have more tarmac roads so maybe travelling will be a bit easier for you."

I wiped the perspiration from my forehead. It wasn't even nine o'clock and the heat was steadily rising.

"Buses can only take a prescribed amount of passengers," Pastor Jack continued, "And passengers have to wear seat belts."

I stifled a chuckle – seat belts on a bus?!

"And the bus drivers have to keep to the speed limit now," he said as we reached the main road and waited for our bus.

I wondered how the government enforced the speed limit – I didn't think they would install speed cameras! Wiping the perspiration from my face again I arranged my bags on the ground and looked around. The traffic was thinning out as most people were at work. There were however, still a number of people walking along the side of the road dressed in varying styles and colours.

The bus arrived not long after nine o'clock and I found everything just as Pastor Jack had said. There were seat belts on each seat and there were no standing passengers. Not so many animals were aboard this bus but the smell of hot bodies and sweat was still overpowering. Once we had left the rutted roads behind and were travelling on a tarmac road, I noticed the difference in the driving. It was indeed a lot smoother and I was just about to ask Pastor Jack if the journey would take less time, when the bus slowed to a halt. Craning my neck to see what was happening, I noticed a uniformed man signalling the bus driver to pull over. I thought perhaps there had been an accident ahead but when I mentioned this to Jack, he laughed.

Puzzled, I watched the official climb aboard the bus and stride up the aisle, checking each person had their seat belt fastened and counting the number of people aboard. He had a quick word with the driver and then departed. The bus started up again and carried on its way.

"So that's how they enforce the new rules," I said to Jack. "Still, it must be quicker with the roads in better condition."

Pastor Jack raised his eyebrows and laughed again. I thought that police checks had been unnecessarily frequent before in my travels in Kenya. Today, the checks were ridiculous. We ended up being stopped nearly every half hour and the driver seemed to be a bag of nerves. I estimated that without the checks, we could have taken at least an hour off the journey, but at the rate we were going it might even take longer than usual.

In the heat, the tarmac was dry, but by the sides of the roads I could see great patches of mud caused by the torrential rain that had been pouring down during the last few nights. We entered the hills and despite spotting the usual Kenyan wildlife, I was getting a bit bored with the checks. I was just thinking to myself that all the fun had gone out of travelling in Kenya, when the bus swerved suddenly into the side of the road. I could feel the mud slip beneath the wheels and felt slightly disorientated as the bus swung round. The vehicle came to a halt and I could clearly see the inspector waving at us from the road. The front wheels of the bus were still resting on the roadway and most of the body of the bus was across the mud at the side of the road. However, the rear wheels, and our seats were hanging over the edge of the road and looking down I realised there was a very long drop.

I've got to get out! was my immediate reaction. But no one moved. I swallowed hard and looked at Pastor Jack who was listening to the driver.

"Come on Monica," Jack said when the driver had finished speaking, "We've got to get out and try to move the bus back onto the road."

I concurred with that sentiment entirely and hastily unfastened my seatbelt.

"What happened?" I asked Pastor Jack as we trooped slowly off the bus with the other passengers.

"I think the driver overreacted when the inspector signalled him to pull over," was Jack's reply.

Overreacted? I thought. *That guy just nearly killed us. Perhaps travelling in Kenya wasn't so boring after all.*

I stood with the women passengers while the men tried to push the bus back onto the road. The vehicle didn't budge an inch and the men got rather muddy. Renewing their efforts, the men got the bus moving but not onto the road. At one point I thought the bus was going to fall backwards down the side of the hill. Just then a large lorry travelling towards Nairobi hooted us and came to a halt. The sides of the lorry were covered in red dust and mud and there were vast patches of rust evident. The men driving the lorry produced a towing rope and fixed it to the front of the bus. The first time they tried pulling the bus back onto the road, the rope slipped off and my heart sank. Undeterred, they tried again and this time the bus slowly rolled onto the road.

Back in the bus again I told myself that I didn't mind the journey being boring. Then I realised how bad it could have been and silently thanked God for keeping us safe.

We finished travelling by bus at Siaya and took a taxi to Obambo village. I arranged for the taxi to return to Obambo in the morning to take me back to Siaya as I needed to buy pens and paper. We reached Obambo in the dark and my eyes were heavy by the time the taxi stopped.

I was used to the heavy rain in Kenya and fell asleep that night with the sound of water drumming on the tin roof resounding in my ears. Towards morning I woke suddenly, aware of the steady tattoo of rain above me. I lay there for a while, wondering why I was awake when I was so desperately tired still. Realising why I felt uncomfortable, I groaned quietly. The toilet was a long way from Jack's hut and I could imagine the mud and water that lay between me and my destination. Sighing, I got out of bed, pulled a cardigan over my pyjamas and found my shoes and glasses. I tiptoed through the hut without disturbing anyone and braced myself for the rain.

It was warm and humid and I didn't feel chilled at all. What took my breath away was the sheer force of the rain on my body. When I tried to walk I found I was slipping and sliding in thick, glutinous mud. In the pitch dark I couldn't see where I was going and even if I had been able to see objects, the rain soon covered my glasses. I knew I had to go around Jack's hut and then I would be on the path to the toilet. Stepping as carefully as I could through the mud I inched forwards. Growing more confident, even as the rain continued to batter me, I walked a little faster and a little faster with the mud clinging to my shoes and seeping down the sides, covering my feet. Then I tripped on a rut beneath the slippery mud and measured my length on the ground. A clanging noise and a shock of cool water in my face made me push myself upright immediately. Feeling on the ground like a blind woman, I discovered a metal bowl beside the wall of Jack's hut that had been full of rainwater. At that moment the dogs started barking. My heart contracted in fear, adrenalin shooting through my body and I found myself standing upright. I couldn't see anything in the darkness and pouring rain, but knew the guard dogs were out there somewhere and that they were barking at me. Feeling thick wetness oozing along my skin as I walked, I tried to ignore the clinging mud and the barking of the dogs, and plodded on down to the toilet. I found the toilet hut and had no more mishaps. I discovered, whilst in the hut, that my glasses were caked in mud. But, as I couldn't see any more without my glasses than with them, muddy as they were, I decided to leave them on – I didn't want to lose them!

My trudge back to Jack's hut through the rain and mud wore me out. At the entrance I found Jack's wife Seline waiting for me with clean water and a cloth. She helped clean me up a bit and I washed my glasses. Once back in my own room I searched for a spare pair of pyjamas and lay down to sleep again – exhausted, but at least nearly dry.

I woke again just after dawn, as Jack's family were waking and I heard the children being sent out for water. The rain had ceased and somewhere in the neighbourhood a rooster was crowing lustily. Wearily I got up and sorted out my wet clothes from my expedition in the rain. Wringing them out as best I could, I hung them up with my dresses suspended from nails in the walls. With all the humidity I wondered how dry my clothes would get. I noticed there was a gap about a foot wide between the top of the wall and the roof and I supposed some kind of breeze must come through.

I was getting dressed when I discovered a large bruise on my right arm. It was tender to touch and quite a nice purple colour. Choosing a dress with sleeves that would cover the bruise, I finished dressing, wondering how on earth I had managed to injure myself like that. All I had done was fall over. I couldn't recall putting my arm out to stop myself from falling. It all happened too quickly for me to even think what to do.

After my ritual wash in hot water, and my breakfast, the taxi from Siaya arrived. As usual, a small crowd of Kenyans were waiting to catch the taxi with me. We bundled in, the front seat reserved for myself and Jack. Already the heat was starting to evaporate the puddles left over from the previous night's torrential rain. We bumped and slithered rather alarmingly from Jack's compound onto the road to Siaya.

I noticed the difference immediately. Usually a car would jolt along over the ruts and struggle through the smaller pot-holes. Today, however, the car seemed to glide. I knew there was no suspension in this particular taxi as we had all been jolted pretty badly as we left Jack's compound. The smoothness of the road was unbelievable, even better than the tarmac roads Jack and I had travelled on yesterday. Staring at the road before us I saw a red, smooth, shiny surface and realised what it was as the car slipped suddenly. Somehow the road had been smoothed out and with all the rain from the night before, the beaten dust track had become a mud rink.

The taxi driver slowed down again at a corner and we slip-slithered around it, going downhill. I found myself gripping onto the edge of my seat, half formed prayers for protection getting wiped from my mind as we slid, instead of drove. Then the road started to climb. The engine roared loudly and the wheels spun and moaned. Pastor Jack and the taxi driver had a brief conversation as the car was put into a lower gear. It rolled forward slightly and then slipped back again. I wondered how the car had reached Obambo in the first place.

Jack said something to the Kenyans crammed on the back seat and they all started getting out of the car. Sliding across the seat I went to follow Jack.

"No, no! Monica, you stay there," he said, "We're going to push the car."

I was going to offer to help but then remembered they considered me a weak, white woman. Staying where I was, I looked up at the road ahead of us and wondered how on earth my friends were going to push the car up so far. Jack called out to the driver who put the taxi into gear and slowly the vehicle edged forwards. Glancing back over the heads of the Kenyans I saw that the road descended behind us at quite a shallow angle, unlike the incline before us. The engine revved and roared as the wheels spun and sucked in the mud. As the car moved slowly up the road the sounds of squelching accompanied our progress. By the time we had reached a level gradient, the men were covered in red mud. I had really wanted to ask what had made the road so smooth but Pastor Jack looked so worn out I hadn't the heart to press him for details.

Despite further slipping and sliding on the way to Siaya we got there safely and my shopping for pens and paper was successful. On the way back to Obambo the road was sticky rather than slippery and I found I wasn't clutching the edge of my seat quite so tightly. I reflected on all the things that had happened in the last twenty-four hours and realised how we'd been protected. So much could have gone wrong yesterday with the bus sliding over the edge of the road. So much could have gone wrong today with the slick mud on the track. I shook my head in amazement and thanked God silently for keeping me and my friends safe. Then I recalled my disastrous trip to the toilet earlier on in the morning. What a fool I'd been falling over and making such a noise! I then realised what the date was. Well, I'd certainly lived up to April Fools Day. Who said God didn't have a sense of humour?!

Friday 2nd to Monday 5th April – Rats!

I was finishing off some notes for the talks I was preparing for my time in Obambo when Pastor Jack disturbed me.

"The children come now Monica," he told me.

"The children?" I asked, putting my notes aside.

"Yes! It is their school holiday now. Some will arrive back home from secondary school today and the rest will be here tomorrow!"

"That's good," I said, wondering exactly how many children's meetings I would be expected to hold and whether some of my previously prepared material could be adapted.

"So you can have a children's meeting this afternoon and another one tomorrow," Jack said generously, "As well as meetings with them every day next week."

"What about the churches in Yimbo you wanted me to visit?"

"Oh there will be plenty of time for everything," he assured me.

I was quite prepared for some children's meetings at some point during my stay in Obambo, but I just hadn't realised how many meetings I would have to run. Certainly Jack had never mentioned school holidays to me! I shrugged to myself as he left the hut. It was the Kenyan way and I would have to prepare as much as I could and leave the rest to God. I was all prepared for the adults' meetings – I had planned a series taking them through the Lord's Prayer. I even had some prepared material for the children going through the events of Easter week with them. What could I do for the meeting today and tomorrow though?

I was suddenly prompted to look up some notes I had tucked away in one of my bags about the glory of God and heaven. Reading through them I saw how relevant they would be as a precursor to the teaching I had for the children during Easter week. Furthermore, I saw that a brief overview today, wouldn't make the children who arrived tomorrow feel left out. Adding a few more notes to the existing sheet, I started going through the points in more detail.

In the evening I felt exhausted. The first children's meeting had gone really well. The children had been well behaved as usual and, despite the fact that they were on holiday now, were eager to learn more about God. We had had a brief but violent downpour as we sat down to eat supper together in Jack's hut. Now the rain had ceased again and just the occasional drip-drip punctuated the animated talk once the meal was over.

"The micro financing is doing really well," Jack told me. "By the end of this year we will have made thirty per cent profit!"

Their ventures included buying and selling old clothes, as well as growing cabbages and cereal crops such as maize and millet. I was thinking about the good harvest they had had when I went to bed that night. As I was drifting off to sleep I thought I heard a rustle nearby. Holding my breath, I heard nothing. Relaxing and letting sleep steal over me, I heard the sound again. Even though it was pitch dark I opened my eyes and stared around, wondering if something was there in the gap between the top of the wall and the roof. After that I heard nothing and fell asleep.

I woke again in the night, hearing the same rustling sound. Only this time it was accompanied by running noises on the roof above me. And it wasn't the sound of running water. These were footsteps of four-legged creatures. I swallowed hard and strained my ears listening for any sounds inside my room. Deciding that I needed to visit the compound toilet, I put on my shoes and cardigan and made my way outside. Overhead a brilliant swollen moon shone down, lighting my way. The earth was only slightly damp and there were no mishaps on my journey to the toilet hut this time. On my way back to Jack's hut however, I saw what I thought were cats running around on the tin roof. As I drew nearer a couple of the creatures stopped running and looked at me.

In the moonlight I could see black, beady eyes and sleek fur coats with long, bald tails. The heads were pointed and the ears were small. I shuddered. Rats! One of them flowed off the roof and into one of the rooms in Jack's hut. I hoped it wasn't mine! On returning to my room and getting into bed again, I realised just where the rat had gone. Behind my room was a room I'd never been in but Jack had told me they stored the maize and millet there. The noises I could hear were the rats feasting on Jack's harvest and then running about on the roof. I really hoped they wouldn't come into my room. Sleep hovered distantly as I listened to the antics of the rats. Slowly I realised that if God could protect me from road accidents, he could certainly protect me from rodents. With that realisation I relaxed and slept.

In the morning I did check my room but there was no evidence the rats had come in. The only creatures I found were a few spiders, most of which measured around two inches. I kept them at a healthy distance and they didn't seem too keen on me either! I started my series on the Lord's Prayer for the adults that day as well as holding the second meeting for the children on the Glory of God and Heaven. On the Sunday I went over the events of Jesus' entry into Jerusalem with the children before the church service started. The children and I had had an excellent time together but I was unprepared for the church service.

Used as I was to exuberant worship and heart felt prayers, I was overwhelmed by the volume and enthusiasm. The church building that I had seen erected three years before was bursting at the seams. So many more people crowded into the wooden building that had first been used the Sunday after Easter in 2001. Afterwards, Pastor Jack confided to me that he would like to erect a brick building next, capable of holding even more people.

It wasn't until the Monday morning, when I was on my way to meet with the children again that I realised what God had done. I was always amazed at the way God answered specific prayers. But this time, God had not even waited to be asked for things. He had just arranged it so that I would be here in Obambo at this specific time to see the church overflowing as well as being able to meet with the children during the day. Pondering on this as the children gathered, I concluded that the longer I walked with God, the more I saw of his provision without even having to ask for it.

Tuesday 6th April – Indignation

The day's teaching was over and I was sitting outside Jack's hut with Jack and his family. The sun was westering and the heat wasn't quite as intense as it had been. I was feeling tired after so much speaking and was thinking that I really ought to go over my notes for the next day. It was far more pleasant to be sitting and talking with my Kenyan friends though. To my surprise a white man suddenly hailed me from the roadway beyond Jack's compound.

All talk ceased as we stared at the newcomer. The man was tall, large and dressed like a businessman.

"Hi!" he said to me, completely ignoring the Kenyans around me. "I'm from Domain," and he indicated the west with his head. "Who are you?"

"I'm Monica Cook," I replied politely, shaking the large hand. "I work for Sunrise Ministries."

"Great!" The Domain man said, grinning at me. He couldn't have heard of Sunrise Ministries. "And where are you staying?"

"Just here," I nodded to the hut behind me.

The grin faltered and the big blue eyes looked troubled. I was beginning to feel I didn't like him – he was still ignoring the Kenyans.

"Sorry, where are you staying?" he asked again.

"Here," I repeated, this time pointing at Jack's hut.

"Right," he seemed uncertain on how to proceed. "How long are you here for?"

"Well, I've been here a week already and I leave for Mombasa on Saturday," I kept my voice pleasant.

The Domain man snorted. "That should be long enough!"

I waited for Jack to say something but he and his family remained silent. The Domain man looked round at the compound, shrugged and said goodbye. When the road had taken him out of sight I turned to Jack.

"Who is he?" I asked, keeping my anger in check, "And what on earth is Domain?"

I felt disgusted at the man's attitude and was really upset that these things had been said in Jack's presence. The family started talking again and preparations for supper were made.

"Domain is an American company," Jack told me quietly. "They are developing the Yala swamp which is about five miles from here. The Yala is a river that starts in the Nandi Hills and runs south of Siaya to flow through the Swamp until it reaches Usengi and the Sea. Many people from Obambo and the surrounding areas have grazed their donkeys and cattle in the swamp for years and years."

"What are they going to do?" I wanted to know, surprised I hadn't been told about this before. "Are they going to build on it?"

Pastor Jack shook his head. "They want to grow rice and aim to produce 80,000 metric tonnes of rice from fifteen hectares. The reason they've been allowed to do it is because they've promised employment."

"How much employment?" I questioned.

"Well, 175 of the 182 staff will be employed from the local area."

"Obambo is the local area?"

"No, the area next to us – they will get the jobs."

"What about all the people who graze their donkeys and cattle in the swamp?" I queried.

Pastor Jack shrugged, indicating there was nothing anyone could do. "They all lose their livelihoods."

"And how many people have donkeys and cattle?"

"Thousands."

"So 175 staff doesn't really make up for thousands!" I felt really angry with Domain.

"But," said Jack, "The whole Siaya area will benefit – and we will too, indirectly. Domain has promised schools, tarmac roads, piped water and good hospitals."

"That's all very well," I said dryly, "but what kind of a company is Domain?"

"It's a large company with good shares, so I've been told."

"But they're not necessarily doing all this for the good of the people already here," I pointed out. "They're probably just concerned with the extension of their own profit."

Pastor Jack shrugged again in that way that indicated passive acceptance of the inevitable. "We might also get electricity through here too."

I thought for a moment. "So is that why the road is now smooth?" I asked. "Are they preparing for it to be covered in tarmac?"

Jack nodded. "They have a large vehicle which has a roller and a scraper to smooth out the ruts in the road. It makes travel quicker." His face darkened for a moment. "We get too many vehicles now driving too fast on the road – lots of animals have been killed, including one of my oxen."

My heart sank. The oxen had been bought with money donated from England. I almost asked about compensation but one look at Jack's face made me hold my tongue.

"Do the children still play in the road?" I asked hesitantly after a while.

Pastor Jack nodded. "But thank God none of them have been hit." His unspoken "yet" hung in the air between us.

I knew forgiveness didn't always come easily, but I struggled that night to forgive the Domain Company for their treatment of the Kenyans. What amazed me was the passivity of my friends. They were almost fatalistic about the Americans taking over. I wanted to raise a protest and stop the Americans. But I knew that was not the way God wanted it to be. If the Kenyans were content to let things happen, then I should leave well alone. I fell asleep still thinking of the thousands of donkey and cattle owners who wouldn't be able to graze their animals at the swamp from September.

Wednesday 7th April – Maasai Trouble

As I was leaving on Saturday, I had to compress my talks to the children on the events of Easter week and ended up speaking about the Last Supper on the Wednesday. I finished both adult and children's meetings and, as I had some more talks to prepare for my trip to Yimbo with Jack on Thursday, I was busy reading notes and making points for these sessions sitting in Pastor Jack's hut. The heat inside was just more bearable than the heat outside even though it was nearly evening. All at once the dogs in the compound started barking. That set off the dogs in the nearby area and then I heard the awful noise of people shouting at the tops of their voices. Leaving my notes on the floor I peered out of the hut to see what looked like the whole of Obambo on the roadway outside the compound. They were moving in a group towards Jack's "next door" neighbour's plot.

Nervously I hurried across the compound, climbed down into the ditch that now separated the compound from the road and up onto the road itself. Being at the back of the crowd I couldn't see anything much as we surged up to the wooden gates that marked the entrance to the government official's land. To my astonishment the crowd climbed over the gates, shouting and calling at the tops of their voices. I stopped at the gates and being tall, could see over.

On the beaten earth before the western style house stood four men. The crowd from Obambo milled around just inside the gates, shouting continuously. I only recognised one man out of the four in front of the house and that was Jack. He stood with his back to two Kenyans who looked both angry and scared. All three of them were facing a tall, fierce-looking Kenyan carrying a spear with a club in his belt. He had a bow on his back and arrows in a quiver at his waist. This tall man was shouting at the two Kenyans behind Jack and I felt a shock of fear. Even though I didn't understand the language, I felt sure the tall man was threatening the other two Kenyans with death.

Pastor Jack raised his hands in a placating manner and spoke in a normal voice to the tall man who listened and then replied. Turning to the two Kenyans behind him, Jack spoke to them urgently. They replied in a babble of noise as the Obambo crowd increased their angry calls. Jack spoke again to the tall man who handed over something small to the Pastor who then passed it on to the Kenyans. Without looking back the two Kenyans ran around the side of the house and vanished.

I noticed the tall man glancing sideways at the crowd and his nostrils flared. Pastor Jack spoke to him and then turned to the crowd. But it was too late. As one the crowd surged forwards a couple of steps and the tall man raised his spear threateningly. The crowd swayed and hesitated. Taking his chance, the tall man ran and the crowd started after him. Pastor Jack raised his arms and shouted and the crowd lost momentum, swirling in a riot of colour and angry black faces. At Jack's urgings the crowd climbed the gates and returned to their homes. Jack was the last one over the gate and he looked very weary.

"Are you all right Monica?" he asked.

I nodded quickly to reassure him. "What happened?"

"I'm sorry I couldn't let you know what was happening," he said, ignoring my question. "But it was a very delicate situation."

"That's all right," I told him. "But I want to know what was going on! I thought you or the other Kenyans might have got killed at one point."

We climbed down into the ditch off the road and hauled ourselves up into Jack's compound. I frowned. That was another thing Jack wouldn't complain about. The "road smoother" made access difficult, creating ditches. I shook my head slightly to keep myself concentrated on the more pressing need to know what had happened. We sat down in Jack's hut and rested for a moment.

"As you know," Jack began. "The house next to us belongs to a government official who is hardly ever there. He had employed two men from Obambo to look after the house, grounds and animals and they'd been doing this for a long time."

I nodded, having heard snippets about the official next door on my previous visits to Obambo.

"However, a few days ago the official employed a Maasai warrior to look after his cattle. The Maasai are cattle specialists you know."

I didn't, but filed that bit of information away for future use.

"The Maasai warrior had taken the cattle out first thing this morning and brought them back just now," Jack continued. "When he arrived at the house he was confronted by the two men from Obambo who work in the house and grounds. They were angry because the Maasai warrior had locked up every room in the house so they couldn't even get into their own rooms there, let alone do their work."

"Why did he do that?" I asked.

Jack smiled. "According to the Maasai warrior, his employer had told him to lock everything up when he went out with the cattle." He sighed. "By the time I got between them, things had gone too far and the Maasai warrior was ready to kill. I managed to persuade him to let the other two workers go and he gave me the key. I told them to get their things and leave and I doubt they'll ever go back there."

"It was pretty frightening," I told him. "I thought the tall man was threatening to kill the others."

"He could have done it," Jack told me. "Maasai warriors are fighters. He had his spear and club and his arrows were poisoned."

I shivered, even though the heat was intense. "Why did the warrior run away at the end then?"

"He was frightened he'd be overwhelmed by the mob I expect."

"He'll be back though, won't he?" I wanted to know.

"Of course!" Jack grinned suddenly. "He is Maasai!"

Jack got called away then and as I tidied up my notes I thought about what he'd told me. I hadn't realised the Maasai were quite so fierce and ready to kill when I'd arranged to visit the Maasai tribes around Narok! *Are you sure you still want me to go there Lord?* I asked silently as I put my notes away in my room. Then I realised I was being silly. The Maasai warrior out there today had been under threat. I was going to meet other Maasai people under different circumstances.

Thursday 8th to Sunday 11th April – The Luggage Rack

As always my last few days in Obambo flew past. On the Thursday I accompanied Pastor Jack to Yimbo where we met with five churches that came under the umbrella of the Victorious Christian Church. I brought my notes and gave them talks on the subjects I'd prepared. What really impressed me though about these five churches was their respect for Jack. Pastor Jack led the Victorious Christian Church and oversaw many other churches, not just these five. None of the churches we met with that day belonged to any particular denomination, they were just unaffiliated indigenous churches. There was no sense of "what can we get out of this?" in the meetings. The churches were genuine in their desire for Pastor Jack's wisdom and counsel. As they all listened with utmost respect to Jack's comments and decisions, I saw a different side to Jack that I'd not seen before.

On Good Friday I covered the events up to and including the resurrection as I didn't want the children to miss out on anything. At the end of the teaching sessions, the children and I had a party. I had brought some balloons over from England and together we blew them up and took them outside where the children started playing with them. I noticed the sky seemed veiled and without warning a hot wind blew down, swirling red dust into our eyes and mouths. Such was the force of the wind that many of the balloons were torn out of the children's hands and set free to tumble over and over as they disappeared in the dust storm. Ushering the children back inside the church building, I noticed some of the younger ones crying. The older children thought the wind and the balloons had been great fun and as we brushed the red dust out of our clothes and wiped our faces clean, I thought of a way of comforting the little ones.

"It is a shame you didn't have long to enjoy your balloons," I said in the quiet. "But you could think of the balloons as your prayers to God. You pray and just as the wind swept your balloons away, your prayers go up to God who hears every word."

The tears dried on the faces of the smaller children, though I could see that most of them would have preferred to play with their balloons for longer. The older children carried on laughing and talking about the event all the way into suppertime and beyond.

The following day Pastor Jack and I, along with the usual compliment of Obambo people hitching a lift, took a taxi to Siaya. I felt sad to be leaving Obambo but at the same time felt excited as I still had three and a half weeks left in Kenya. We took a bus from Siaya, which initially was quite uncomfortable. We got on board with the other passengers, paid for our seats and then discovered that the luggage rack on one side of the bus was damaged. Pastor Jack shrugged as the driver shouted over the conversations in the bus.

"He says we can't use it Monica," Jack told me as I was about to haul one of my heavy suitcases up onto the rack.

"What are we going to do with it?" I asked, looking at my cases and hand luggage.

I had my hand luggage on my lap in the end and we managed to partially wedge one suitcase under the seat. The other suitcase had to stand in the aisle with Pastor Jack preventing it from falling over.

"Are you certain this isn't illegal?" I joked, gesturing at all the luggage in the aisle.

Pastor Jack shrugged again. "Apparently the luggage rack will be mended in Kisumu."

Well, I thought, Siaya to Kisumu wasn't too far to travel like this. As soon as the bus started up and moved off I realised that in fact, Siaya to Kisumu was a very long way indeed. The luggage rack was loose and bounced up and down as the bus travelled along the road. I eyed the jumping metal rack nervously. It wasn't going to fall on us, was it? Not only was the rack dangerous, it was also noisy. It rattled and screeched and jangled and wore on our ears. Conversation was impossible and combined with the lack of space because of the luggage on the floor, made for exceedingly uncomfortable travelling conditions.

The passengers on the bus breathed an audible sigh of relief as the bus jolted to a halt outside a large brick building somewhere on the outskirts of Kisumu. Silence fell like a blessing for a moment and then those who were disembarking moved out.

"What is this place?" I asked Jack as we stood up, moved the luggage aside and went out to stretch our legs.

"It's a bus depot," he said. "The buses stop here for oil and petrol. And there's the mechanic who will mend the rack."

A tired-looking Kenyan man climbed on board the bus carrying a welder and a piece of cardboard box. Intrigued, Jack and I watched him through the window. I felt a bit too hot in the sun but when the mechanic started welding, I was glad to stay outside. Sparks flew everywhere as he fixed the luggage rack and I noticed that he'd put the piece of cardboard over a seat.

"Why's he put cardboard over that seat?" I asked Jack.

"To protect it, I think," was his reply.

At that moment a shower of red-hot sparks fell on the cardboard, catching it alight. Automatically Jack and I backed off from the window as the mechanic stopped welding. Knocking the cardboard to the floor he stamped on the flames and put out the smouldering fabric of the seats. By that time the bus had filled with smoke and the mechanic stumbled out, coughing. When the smoke had cleared he went back in and finished repairing the luggage rack. By the time we boarded the bus again the air still smelt of smoke.

The rest of the journey was uneventful, in comparison to previous Kenyan journeys. We were stopped many times by the police but the bus driver this time was quite confident and not as nervous as the driver who had driven us up from Nairobi to Siaya. We arrived at the slums outside Nairobi quite late in the evening and found our way to Sylvester's house. In the morning we went to Sylvester's church and I found it strange to be celebrating Easter again so soon after my time with the children in Obambo on Friday. Strange, but good!

PART TWO – MOMBASA

See I am sending an angel ahead of you to guard you along the way and to bring you to the place I have prepared. (Exodus 23:20)

Monday 12th April – Mombasa Airport

Outside Nairobi Airport I said goodbye to Pastor Jack and the members of Sylvester's church who had come along to see me off.

"Now Monica," said Pastor Jack. "I want you to have this," and he handed me a mobile phone. "If you get any problems in Mombasa, just call me. My mobile number is programmed into the phone."

I was speechless. I didn't even know Pastor Jack had a mobile phone!

"Just make sure you call me when you reach Mombasa," he continued. "And call me again when you have met up with your contact."

"Yes!" I found my voice. "Of course I will!"

Still surprised and touched by Jack's generosity, I entered the airport, automatically checking the times of my flight. The flight to Mombasa was short and uneventful, though I did have time to reflect on how predictable Pastor Jack's concern for me was. It wasn't that he didn't trust the other Christians I was going to be with. No, not at all. I think he felt I was his guest in Kenya and if anything happened to me, he would be the one at fault.

Having been to many different airports in the world, nothing stood out particularly about the one at Mombasa, except that there seemed to be more seats and tables around. I was not the only white person travelling to Mombasa. Hordes of holidaymakers from all parts of Europe were constantly passing through the airport, being met by people from the hotels they had booked. The airport building was full of Kenyans holding placards with the names of the different hotels on them. Droves of travellers flocked to "their" hotel and were then escorted outside. I looked around for a placard with my name on it. Nothing. The placards started to disappear and the crowds began to thin. Now the taxi drivers pressed forward, offering their services.

"Where do you want to go?" one Kenyan asked me.

"I don't know," I said, feeling stupid. "My lift hasn't arrived yet."

At that moment the mobile Jack had given me, rang. Hurriedly I pulled it out of my hand luggage as the taxi driver wandered off to a more likely looking fare.

"Hello?" I said.

"Monica! It's Jack!"

I nearly laughed with relief.

"Are you all right?" he sounded very concerned.

"I'm fine," I told him. "I've just arrived and am trying to find my lift."

"Well, you take care and call me when your lift does arrive."

"I will!" I promised and Jack terminated the call.

"Where do you want to go?" asked another taxi driver.

"I'm waiting for a lift," I replied.

I'd told a dozen taxi drivers the same story when I realised the airport was nearly deserted and I stuck out like a sore thumb. Just as vultures circle and descend on a corpse, so the taxi drivers, returning from their earlier fares, started circling me.

"Why don't you call your contact," one of them suggested, "Find out where she is and then one of us can take you there."

I wondered why I hadn't thought of that before. Sitting down on one of the empty seats nearby, I fished out my notebook from my hand luggage and found my contact's telephone number. It was a mobile number and I wondered, as I punched the numbers in, how much money was on my phone.

"Hello, Miriam?" I asked as the phone was answered. "It's Monica Cook here!"

"Oh hello Monica!" came Miriam's voice, somewhat distorted. "How are you?"

"I'm OK," I told her. "I'm at Mombasa Airport and no-one's turned up yet to meet me!"

"Oh!" Miriam sounded surprised. "I did ask someone to pick you up, but I can't remember if he said he could or was going to organise someone else to collect you."

The distortion on the phone together with Miriam's accent made it very difficult to understand her.

"Where are you?" I asked her. "Are you in Mombasa?"

"No!" was her cheerful reply. "I'm at a children's camp about one and a half hour's drive away."

My heart sank.

"Where do you want me to go?" I asked. "I'm supposed to be doing training, aren't I this week?"

"That's all changed," Miriam said. "You're to be with me at this camp now and do some training next week."

My brain went into overdrive. All that preparation I'd done! I thought I was training this week and then using the people I'd trained to reach out to the children at the camp that was happening next week. Everything was turning upside down.

"So, how do I get to this camp?"

"Let me see if someone can pick you up first, I've got your number and I'll call you back."

I replaced the mobile in my bag as another horde of holidaymakers poured into the airport building. Whilst I'd been talking to Miriam the placard holders had been assembling. The taxi drivers stopped circling as new fares were evident. I scanned the placards quickly hoping in vain to see my name. Then I sat down, feeling a bit depressed. All my plans were in disarray. And Miriam hadn't said when she would ring back. The mobile rang, its shrill tones piercing the chaos around me. Thinking it was Miriam I snatched it up and answered it.

"Monica!" It was Jack. "Where are you?"

"Same place," I replied.

"Why? What's happened?"

"No-one's here to pick me up!"

"What about your contact?"

"Oh I've rung Miriam but she's going to call me back."

"When?"

"She didn't say."

"You are OK though aren't you?"

"Fine thanks Jack. I'll let you know when someone arrives for me."

I didn't think things were looking very good but somehow I wasn't panicking. I felt that peace inside me that indicated that God had everything under control. Even the reversal of the teaching and training in Mombasa wasn't really a problem. I glanced at my watch. I'd been waiting for just over one hour.

Similar patterns of movements and questions emerged over the next two hours. The droves of travellers made regular appearances and in between the incoming flights, the taxi drivers would circle closer and closer. I tried ringing Miriam again and again but she was either engaged or my mobile couldn't get a signal. There was one taxi driver who seemed a little more trust worthy than the others, who kept going outside and keeping a watch for my lift. Jack rang two more times, practically on the hour. After Jack had rung the fourth time, the airport was slowly clearing of holidaymakers and I found I was sitting next to a large Kenyan lady who was obviously waiting for someone. I had just put the mobile back into my bag when it rang again.

"Monica! It's Miriam!"

I almost cried with relief. "Hello!" I managed cheerily.

"You must take a taxi!" Miriam said.

"I will as soon as they return," I said. "There's no-one around at the moment. Where do I have to go?"

"Take a taxi to . . . Church," said Miriam, static and her accent preventing me from understanding her. "It's on the corner of . . . Area."

"Sorry!" I found myself shouting into the phone whilst scrabbling in my bag for notebook and pencil. "Where do I go?"

Miriam repeated the address but I couldn't understand it.

"Hold on a moment!" I shouted at her and turned to the Kenyan lady next to me. "Please could you tell me what she is saying?" I asked.

The lady nodded and took the phone from me. She listened intently and then repeated the address slowly for me. "Mombasa Pentecostal Church on the corner of Jomo Kenyatta Avenue."

I wrote the address down and took the phone back from her.

"I'm a born again Christian!" she announced. "And so is he!" She pointed to a taxi driver approaching us.

"Thank you Miriam," I said, "I'll take a taxi there."

I had no idea if the lady sitting next to me really was a born again Christian or even if the taxi driver waiting in front of me was one either. Miriam said I needed a taxi and it looked as though I had a taxi driver. I just had to trust God and my new companions. As we got in the taxi and the driver piled my luggage in the boot, he asked the born again lady if it was north or south coast I wanted. When she asked me, I just shrugged, I had no idea what they were talking about. The sun was sinking towards the west as we drove through Mombasa, rich in its hotels and tropical foliage.

At length we arrived at Mombasa Pentecostal Church, clearly marked by lettering on its walls. The shadows were long I noticed as I got out of the car and knocked on the door. I waited but no one answered. Trying the door I discovered it was locked and despair washed through me. Getting back into the car I reached for my bag and mobile when the sound of someone running drew my attention back to the street.

"Is this who you are waiting for?" the Kenyan lady asked.

I looked around and saw a young Kenyan slowing down beside the church.

"Hello!" he panted. "I'm Simon. Miriam sent me to meet you Monica!"

I wanted to ask him so many things such as where am I going? Where is Miriam? Who exactly are you? Just what is going on? But I didn't have a chance. Simon was negotiating with the taxi driver to take both of us to the Word of Life Centre. When the Kenyan lady heard that, she announced she was going back to the airport and went off to find another taxi. By the time Simon got in the taxi and we drove off again, I was feeling very tired and very confused.

I suddenly remembered that I hadn't rung Pastor Jack to let him know what was happening. He answered the phone immediately.

"Where are you Monica?" he asked before I could say anything.

"I'm in a taxi with someone called Simon who's taking me to meet Miriam at the Word of Life Centre," I told him wearily.

"Oh good!" he sounded relieved.

I said goodbye, switched the mobile phone off and glanced out of the window. Night sprang up suddenly as the sun disappeared and it became hard to distinguish features from the townscape around us.

I became aware of the road sloping down towards something dark shot with bright colour that constantly moved. Ahead of us was a jetty that allowed the driver to take the car straight onto a boat.

"Are we going by ferry?" I asked a little nervously.

"Yes," replied Simon, "It is the likoni – the ferry."

Still feeling very confused, I wondered why I had come to Mombasa, only to now leave the island. The ferry trip was short and then we were out in the wilds of Kenya once more.

"How far is it to the Word of Life Centre?" I asked Simon wearily.

"Only about one and a half hours' drive," was his reply.

Only! I thought to myself. What a strange day I was having. At least though my destination sounded biblical!

Tuesday 13th to Monday 19th April – Word of Life Centre

The Word of Life Centre was situated beside the sea and I woke to the sound of surf as bright sunlight penetrated my room. Sitting in the "dining room" – a large thatched building – I ate my breakfast enjoying the view and feeling relaxed. I had heard a high pitched chattering noise ever since I had woken up and assumed that it was some kind of bird making the sound. As I ate, the chattering increased and without warning the piece of bread I was holding in my hand, vanished. Turning round I saw a little grey-brown monkey running away with my bread in its mouth! I was so shocked I didn't even try and run after it. At that moment a Kenyan lady walked in.

"Hi Monica!" she smiled warmly. "I'm Miriam." Now we were face-to-face I could understand her accent.

Still feeling a bit off balance by having my breakfast stolen by a monkey, I managed to greet Miriam.

Children's camp at the Word of Life Centre, Mombasa

"OK," she said and proceeded to outline the plan for the week as if there had been no other plan ever discussed. "There are fifty six children on this camp and you will be doing the main teaching."

"How old are they?" I asked, wondering if I had prepared enough material for so many children.

"They're seven to fourteen," Miriam replied. "We split them up into seven-to ten year olds and eleven-to-fourteen year olds. We also separate the boys from the girls for some subjects such as sex education."

Sex education? I wasn't prepared for that! She must have seen the look on my face as she laughed.

"We have outside speakers coming in to talk about that," Miriam reassured me. "We try to combine lifestyle choices with holy living. Now, we had intended to give you a break today as you must be tired from all the travelling." I nodded, wondering how much they wanted me to do. "There's a lady here with the under elevens now. She was due to teach them this afternoon as well but she has to go at lunchtime. Can you take them this afternoon?"

"Yes of course," I said and racked my brains to work out what to do with them.

"The others here aren't experienced enough to take on a teaching session at such short notice," Miriam explained. "You will have them for about two hours."

Two hours! Back in my room I went through my luggage. Pens and paper always came in useful. And there were still lots of balloons left in one bag so I took them with me as well. I tidied my room and prayed. The irritation and annoyance with the change of plan and disorganisation disappeared. I realised that this was how God wanted it to be.

In the afternoon I took my group of under-elevens down to the beach of white sand and held a sandcastle building competition. The scenery was idyllic. White sand, blue water, sun blazing out of a tropical sky. The only fly in the ointment was the wind, which tore along in great hot gusts, swirling loose sand into our eyes. Once the sandcastles were finished we sat down together on the warm sand and talked about building houses on rock and sand and what that meant to us. Then I talked to the children about the storm on the Lake of Galilee, which seemed rather ironic to me as the weather was perfect for a holiday! I likened the storm on the lake to storms in the children's lives, which they readily understood. When I gave them each a piece of paper they quickly wrote down the things they considered storms. We placed each piece of paper into a balloon, blew the balloons up and ended the afternoon with a balloon game. A few balloons burst prematurely and the gusting wind made things a little difficult. But right at the end, the remaining balloons were burst and we all prayed about each other's storms.

The teaching I brought that week was well received and fifteen children had made a commitment to Jesus by the time the camp finished. And I learnt a couple of things

Children at the Word of Life Centre

about Kenya that I had not known before. I had been aware that Kenyans always covered themselves up. They did not show much flesh at all. I discovered, from conversations amongst the Kenyan staff and teachers at the camp that generally Kenyans found the sight of sunbathing tourists quite disgusting. They saw it as white people showing their bodies off and it was worse if they were fat! When tourists walked around in shorts and bikinis the Kenyans thought it was dreadful, and if the tourists were sunburnt that was worse – who would want to look like a lobster? I found this amusing – seeing Europeans from the point of view of the Kenyans.

I also discovered, first hand, how difficult it was to get any medical help at short notice. Saturday was the last day of the camp and Mary, a lady from New Zealand, had been visiting the Word of Life Centre that day. Mary had been listening in on some of my teaching and while the children were sent off to collect their things before they left the Centre, she and I talked about the camp. Mary suddenly went very white and her eyes became slightly glazed.

"Are you all right?" I enquired.

"I think I'm going to throw up," she said faintly.

"The toilets are upstairs," I told her. "Would you like me to help you up there?"

"No, no thank you, I can make it," and Mary walked slowly to the stairs.

I started clearing up my materials and notes, wondering where I would be going next as I put things away in my room. After a while I began to feel uneasy about Mary and went to see if she had returned from the toilets. None of the Centre staff had seen her and feeling worried, I rushed upstairs. When I entered the ladies' toilets the stench of vomit nearly made me retch. Holding my breath I looked around for Mary. I found her collapsed in front of a toilet pan and there was vomit everywhere.

"Mary?" I whispered and she mumbled something at me. "I'm going to get help," I told her.

As fast as I could I returned downstairs, praying the whole time. The Centre staff were cleaning up as I appeared and looked rather startled at my request.

"Where's the nearest doctor?" I wanted to know.

They looked bemused and shrugged.

"It's Mary," I started to babble, "She's collapsed in the toilets, she's very sick. She's needs a doctor."

"We don't know any doctors round here," said one of the staff. "We don't live here."

"But there must be a surgery or something!"

The Kenyans looked at each other and shrugged again.

"This is really serious," I tried to get across to them that this was an emergency. "Mary could be dying."

"There might be a doctor in Mombasa," said someone else.

"What about a hospital?" I asked. "What would the phone number be?"

I had Jack's mobile phone, I remembered. If we could

find a number . . . One look at their faces killed that idea. This wasn't England with its emergency services and Yellow Pages.

"Is there a vehicle around?" I asked. "Then we could take Mary to hospital!"

"We only have one vehicle here," the staff told me. "It's gone to pick up petrol so the children can be taken back to Mombasa."

A wave of helplessness poured over me. There seemed nothing I could do.

"I'll get some sheets," said one of the female staff and disappeared.

At that moment the sound of a van engine chugging along reached our ears. Before I could ask someone to go and stop it, the sound stopped near the Centre. Not quite believing my eyes I hurried out to see a large van with a Kenyan driver.

"We've got to take a lady to hospital," I called. "Can you take us?"

The Kenyan driver didn't seem surprised. He nodded in agreement and got out of his van. Thinking I would have his help in getting Mary down the stairs I hurried inside again, the feeling of helplessness receding. The woman with the sheets accompanied me upstairs as did the other female members of staff. Poor Mary was still vomiting while we wrapped her in the sheets. Someone found a bucket from somewhere, which helped a bit.

"We'd better get the men to carry her," I suggested when Mary was wrapped up.

The Kenyan women looked shocked.

"They couldn't do that," the woman with the sheets told me. "It would be wrong."

Wrong? I thought. How can helping someone be wrong? I didn't argue with their culture and so we half walked, half carried Mary down the stairs between us. We were all out of breath by the time we reached the van as Mary was not small and in her semi conscious state was pretty much a dead weight. We got her into the van and laid her down on one of the seats in the back, which was about three seats in width. Thanking the staff at the Centre, I held Mary down on the seat as the driver put the van in gear and we drove away. The drive seemed endless to me but I discovered later that the hospital wasn't that far away at all. On arrival the driver got the hospital staff to take Mary into the hospital where questions about medical insurance were asked. It turned out Mary had medical insurance so she was put onto a drip and given injections. In a relatively short time she perked up and I stayed with her until she was out of danger. When I left the hospital, the Kenyan and his van had disappeared. I took a bus back to the Centre by myself and discovered on arrival that not only had all the children gone, but that there were no staff there either!

I slept that night by myself. I felt somewhat apprehensive about it but trusted God to look after me. I woke feeling refreshed in the morning and waited a while for a bus to take me to the hospital. The trip to the hospital in the daylight was certainly more pleasant than the nightmare drive of the evening before. Mary was much recovered, though she'd been told she had to stay in the hospital for the weekend. It turned out she'd had both malaria and food poisoning, but she was out of danger now. Her medical insurance had saved her life. If she had been a Kenyan she probably wouldn't have been treated.

On my return to the Centre, I found Miriam there with a friend of hers – Mildred. Mildred was a short Kenyan woman with a lovely smile. I found out quite soon though that despite her smile, she could be incredibly tough. Miriam and Mildred stayed with me that night and in the morning we took a taxi to visit Mary in hospital. She was due to be released later that day and was intending to return to Nairobi as soon as she could. When we came out of the hospital, Miriam and Mildred suggested we took a matatu to The Word of Life Centre. A matatu was a small local bus taking between twelve to fifteen people, making short journeys. We had a pleasant ride to the Centre and when we got off we paid our fare. Miriam was first and was charged ten shillings. Mildred was also charged ten shillings. But when I handed over ten shillings the driver wanted to charge me sixty! I refused and got out of the matatu at Miriam's signal.

"It's because you're white, Monica," Miriam started to say to me when two men got off the matatu and started towards us.

It happened so quickly I reacted instinctively. The two Kenyan men started to punch the three of us. The punches hurt and our hats were quickly knocked off. Short little Mildred leapt up and grabbed the tallest man's hat. They were pummelling away at us and we were hitting them back, trying to fight them off. Out of the corner of my eye I saw people walking by and looking at us but no one interfered. It felt like for ever but suddenly the punching ceased. The tall man asked Mildred for his hat back and she handed it over to him and then whacked him really hard on the shoulder. He ran back to the matatu, followed by his companion.

"Come on Monica!" called Miriam, grabbing my hand and I ran awkwardly after Mildred.

I never did work out why we were fighting. The only explanation I had was Miriam's. Because I was white they charged me more as they thought I had more money. But Miriam was adamant that if the fare cost ten shillings then that was all they could charge.

That evening we left the Word of Life Centre and took a taxi back to Mombasa, using the ferry as before and arrived at Mombasa Pentecostal Church.

Tuesday 20th to Sunday 25th April – Mombasa Pentecostal Church

My second week in Mombasa passed quickly. I stayed at the home of Miriam who lived in the Mikindani area. Not only did she run children's camps at The Word of Life Centre, she was also one of the children's pastors belonging to the Mombasa Pentecostal Church. Sharing her house and meals I had a lot more time to really get to know her during the second week. I learnt that she was originally from Tanzania and was divorced. She had been a Christian for many years and her two children, (the girl was eighteen and the boy twenty), were keen Christians too. Mildred was also staying with Miriam and I learnt that she was engaged to a Kenyan Christian and that they were due to be married at Christmas.

Miriam and Mildred took me to visit two children's homes and accompanied me to my training sessions for children's teachers at the Pentecostal Church. To travel to the children's homes and to the church we had to use the matatus. Fortunately we did not come across the matatu that we'd taken on the way back from hospital on the Monday! Also, I was never charged more than the correct fare for all the journeys I took.

Travelling by matatu was quick and very efficient. The only thing I didn't like about it was getting on. The matatus didn't actually stop at all. They just slowed down enough for people to jump off and jump on. I could swing myself up onto the matatu all right but, due to my hip, I couldn't move forwards very quickly. The matatus had sliding doors and several times I found I was still standing on the threshold of the matatu as it picked up speed and the doors closed on me, leaving my backside sticking out! Miriam explained one evening why the matatus never stopped.

"The drivers get paid for the miles they travel and more for the fares they collect," she said. "That's why they never stop and drive as fast as they can."

In Mombasa, street children were very common and often were extremely young. Part of the work that the Mombasa Pentecostal Church carried out was to build two children's homes outside the city. These were the homes I visited. I went to the boys' home on the Tuesday. It wasn't far to Shika Adabu – we crossed the river by ferry and then drove for half an hour. There were thirty-six boys in the home aged between three and fifteen. They were sponsored by people in the Pentecostal Church to go to school and the home provided food and clothes for them. I noticed some girls amongst the boys and discovered that some poor families pay for their daughters to be fed and taught at the home.

On the Wednesday I travelled in the opposite direction to visit the Wema Centre for girls at Bamburi. We could only take the matatu so far and then we walked the rest of the way to the centre. Here they fed, clothed and educated eighty-five girls between the ages of three and fifteen. The set-up was slightly different here in that the centre arranged for entire families who were very poor to come in and learn a trade. This would enable the poor people to earn money for themselves.

All the children were part of the Pentecostal Church and would come into Mombasa regularly to join in the activities the church ran for children. All the children were keen to listen to what I had to say to them. They got really excited about being taught something and were eager to be involved in whatever activity I was organising. After each meeting, every child wanted my individual attention, which I found quite exhausting. I re-visited the boys' home in Shika Adabu on the Thursday, and then, on the Friday I had a "day off".

I spent Friday morning preparing my notes for the training sessions I was to give the following day. Having been with some of the orphans and homeless children, I altered a few things to make what I said more relevant to the adults I would be teaching. Then in the afternoon I played tourist. At Miriam's suggestion I visited the old town of Mombasa, which was dominated by Muslims. It was a beautiful part of the island with narrow streets full of shops. The buildings on either side were very tall which made the streets seem narrower than they really were. The old town was crowded with people milling around everywhere. Some smart men in suits were sitting outside shops, drinking and talking. I found some material made of a fine cotton in a shop that sold cloth specifically for caftans. This fine cotton was brown and I bought enough to have a caftan made up for me by a friend back in England. I also bought two caftans with intricate embroidery around the neck and cuffs.

On Saturday I trained the teachers not only from the Pentecostal Church, but from other churches in the area too. I was encouraged by their receptivity to my teaching methods – I got them to pretend to be the children and showed them how I would teach children various things. But what really encouraged me was what happened on the Sunday. I was invited to visit the different Sunday School classes that were conducted in the morning and in each class I visited, I found my teaching being put into practice. I was so astonished. The training had finished at 4.00 pm on the Saturday and these classes started at 10.00 am on the Sunday!

Before I left to catch my aeroplane, I said goodbye to Miriam and Mildred and to my delight, Mildred invited me back to Kenya in December 2004 for her wedding!

PART THREE – MAASAI

As the heavens are higher than the earth, so are my ways higher than your ways and my thoughts than your thoughts. As the rain and the snow come down from heaven, and do not return to it without watering the earth and making it bud and flourish, so that it yields seed for the sower and bread for the eater, so is my word that goes out from my mouth; it will not return to me empty, but will accomplish what I desire and achieve the purpose for which I sent it. (Isaiah 55:9–11)

Sunday 25th to Monday 26th April – Europeans!

Still feeling quite buoyant after visiting the Sunday School classes at Mombasa Pentecostal Church, I booked in at the airport at 12.45 for my flight back to Nairobi which was due to leave at 13.45.

"I'm very sorry," said the airport official as he inspected my ticket, "But your flight is delayed. There is something wrong with the aeroplane and the engineers are fixing it now."

"Do you know how long I'll have to wait?" I thought of all the notes I could write up.

The official shrugged. "We don't know," he replied and handed my ticket back to me.

I knew I ought to phone Pastor Jack, otherwise he would be very worried. I tried to call him on the mobile he'd lent me but couldn't get through. I couldn't work out if I hadn't got a signal, hadn't got enough money or had run out of battery. Imagining Jack trying to call me and not getting through, I went to the airport office and asked to borrow their telephone.

I dialled Jack's number and discovered his mobile was on answer phone. I left a message telling him I'd be late and that I wasn't sure what time I'd reach Nairobi.

It wasn't too hot at the airport. The main room, which I felt I knew quite well after my interminable wait before, was relatively cool and airy. There were only a few people waiting around and I had a choice of chairs to sit on. I bought myself a cool drink and a snack, marvelling at the luxuries normally unavailable on such flights. I wrote up all my notes during the afternoon as the room filled up with people waiting for the aeroplane to be mended. As the room became crowded, the noise level rose and it seemed everyone was complaining about having to wait.

"They should have let us know!" one olive-skinned European woman was saying to her husband.

"Well, when I rang the airport yesterday, everything was all right!" snapped the man.

Their children were fractious and noisy and the woman continued to complain in a loud voice. I put my notes away in my hand-luggage thinking to myself that I would rather wait than fly on an aeroplane that might fall to pieces!

At 6.00 pm we were allowed to board the aeroplane and flew to Nairobi. There I was met by Pastor Jack and some of the Nairobi Christians.

"Thank you for your message Monica!" Pastor Jack said and we all exchanged greetings.

"And thank you for the loan of your phone!" I said, handing the mobile back to him.

That evening, in Sylvester's hut, Pastor Jack started talking about a newspaper article he'd seen recently.

"I think it's disgusting that white people go around with no clothes on!" he was saying and I was reminded of the conversations I'd heard at the children's camp.

"It's not just English people," I said in defence of my countrymen. "Some other Europeans strip off too!"

Pastor Jack shook his head. "It's quite offensive," he wrinkled his nose. "To see those white women going around naked. It shouldn't be allowed."

Tuesday 27th to Thursday 29th April – Maasai Highlands

On Tuesday morning I was collected by David Kereto. Whilst waiting for him I felt slightly apprehensive, remembering the aggressive Maasai warrior next door to Pastor Jack in Obambo. As soon as David arrived at about 11.30 am, however, my apprehension disappeared. He was as pleasant and as courteous as Pastor Jack and after saying goodbye to Jack and Sylvester, I went off with David feeling quite relieved. We spoke a little in the car, David telling me about his home and how different the Maasai highlands were to other parts of Kenya. Indeed, the drive up into the hills showed me a face of Kenya I had not yet seen. The colour green dominated everything. The hills were not lush, like Mombasa, but neither were they hard and dry like Obambo. Instead, I could almost have thought I was home in England – except that the heat was intense and the roads were just tracks! Crops grew everywhere and grass clothed the bones of the earth. I sat there amazed.

When we reached David's house, the driver stopped the car outside the compound and I got out. David hurried into the house, calling for his family I assumed. Immediately a girl in her early teens rushed out and stood in front of me looking down at the ground. I stared at her, trying to catch her eye but her head remained bowed. Wondering if there was something wrong with my feet I glanced down at my shoes. Everything was in order – I hadn't stepped in anything. Mystified I turned to the driver who was now getting out of the car.

"She wants you to greet her," he called.

I knew exactly what to do and reached out my hand. Her hand in mine was unresponsive as I shook hands with her. She looked shocked as she raised her head. Wondering what

I'd done wrong, I turned to the taxi driver again but at the moment David returned and my moment of confusion was swallowed up as he introduced me to his family. I learnt that the girl who had greeted me first was not one of David's children but an orphan he and his wife were caring for. David's own children were younger.

As we crossed the compound, David pointed out the various buildings, together with an enclosure for the animals. His cows were eating the grass in the compound and later on they would be herded back into their enclosure for the night. As we entered the house the taxi driver took me aside.

"You should have placed your hand on the girl's head to greet her," he said in a low voice.

"Oh! Thank you!" I said. "I thought the right way to greet someone was to shake their hand."

"In Obambo maybe," the taxi driver smiled. "Maasai are a different tribe. You only shake hands with those who are equal to you. If you are younger then you bow your head."

I gulped, wondering how on earth I would know if someone was equal to me or not. (A few days later I went to a church meeting and a woman who was about thirty took the initiative and shook my hand. I took great encouragement from this as the woman obviously thought I was her age!)

David Kereto's house was wooden and the whole feel of the place was so different from Obambo. The humidity was not so high up in the hills and though it was hot, it was not unbearable. David and I talked a lot that first day.

David had spent some time previously in England at Capernwray in the Lake District as well as spending two years at a college in London. Part of his training at this college involved him being placed at a Kensington church for a while. He came across as being very organised and he obviously had a lot of contacts in the UK. He acted as a pastor to his Maasai community and he was also business orientated. He was very honest and upright and knew exactly what God wanted him to do.

"We have a lot of problems in Kenya," he told me. "And many of the white missionaries were the cause of our problems! The missionaries did all the fishing and didn't teach us Kenyans how to fish."

I nodded slowly, not at all offended by his words, seeing his point.

"So when Kenyans see a white person now they see someone who will supply all their needs. Because this is what the missionaries did! All the Kenyans have to do is beg." He smiled. "You know, we have all the resources we need in Kenya but we don't know how to appropriate them. My mission is to mobilise my people to enable them to get on and develop themselves."

"So how do you do this?" I asked.

"I have contacts in the UK and the US," he replied. "But they are contacts; they do not support my work. I utilise them and learn from them. I am not dependant on them. I want to develop work amongst my tribe – the Maasai – and indeed anyone else in Kenya who is interested! That is why my ministry is called the Maasai Evangelistic Association."

I talked to David about Jack and Obambo, and David's comment was that Jack was a good man. I began to see how David could provide some of the future help for Obambo.

"I have got some medical people coming over from the US shortly," David told me. "They will bring equipment we haven't got and see hundreds of people. But my vision is to provide the Maasai with their own medical help."

"But haven't you got a medical centre already?" I asked.

"Come with me," David said and led me outside.

We stood before the wooden hut designated as the medical centre.

"It is all ready," David told me, "But I cannot open it because I do not have a supply of fresh water yet. Look over there."

He pointed across the grass to a stick some distance away. "That is where the water will be."

"How will you get to the water?" I wanted to know, thinking of Obambo and the borehole.

As we walked back to his house David told me of an American Christian company with an office in Nairobi and an engineer who had quoted him £6,500 for the work. Once we were inside I took down the names and address so I could pass the information on to Pastor Jack. I was amazed at the way God was bringing the right kinds of people together at just the right time. (I did mention the company and engineer to Jack when I saw him next but he was noncommittal. I realised I would have to tread very carefully in this area. Jack would not want David to take over and I knew that David would not do that. There was also the matter of different tribes which is still a problem in Kenya.)

Friday 30th April to Sunday 2nd May – Maasai Plains

Over the next couple of days I travelled around with David, visiting churches and meeting more of the Maasai Christians. I discovered that churches in the Maasai would start under a tree. The local Christians would find a large, shady tree and congregate beneath it until their numbers outgrew the shade of the tree. Then they would build a wooden hut in which to meet and this would be built next to the tree. When their numbers had increased again so that they couldn't all fit into the wooden hut, they would erect a brick building and the wooden hut would be used for children's meetings. I was impressed at the way everything was local and developed quite naturally from, literally, grass root beginnings.

I met many young Maasai people, including boys of sixteen who were about to start training as Maasai warriors for two years. I never found out if it was a tradition or not. The boys were just expected to actively participate in their culture. At

The church at Naisoya – David Kereto's home church

the end of two years they would have the option of returning
to their clan or staying on as a warrior. The warriors were
much respected and they have taken the place of a police force
amongst the Maasai people.

I was present when a friend of David branded their cattle
with their clan marks. The cattle were a sign of wealth
amongst the Maasai and each clan had its own brand. It was
noisy and smelly but very interesting. I felt a bit sorry for the
cattle as the irons were red hot and I could hear the flesh being
scorched. But the cattle seemed to recover quite quickly from
it and didn't appear stressed at all!

On Saturday David took me to the Maasai plains to visit
one of his sisters. Two of his sisters were married to traditional
Maasai tribesmen and one of them lived on the Loita Plain.
We left fairly early in the morning, accompanied by David's
cousin Cyrus. As we drove through the Maasai highlands I
looked around and thought again that if I ignored the road, I
could actually be in England! The neat rows of wheat, barley
and maize in fields either side of the road reminded me of late
spring back home. I saw gangs of Maasai people out in some

Branding cattle in the Maasai

of the fields, taking weeds up by hand. Standing beside some of the compounds we passed were combine harvesters and tractors. The machinery was about thirty years out of date but that just reinforced the old Englishness of the scene.

The track we were following suddenly plunged down a hillside and the driver guided the car around massive boulders. The boulders were just standing on the track and the size of them reminded me of parts of Wales. The track continued to plunge down and then disappeared beneath a stream. I thought perhaps that we would stop and ford the stream in a sedate manner. I was wrong. The driver just kept going and drove through the stream and back up onto the track on the other side. This wasn't a road, I thought to myself, this was an obstacle course!

Shortly after that we joined a wide, tarmac road and followed it for about thirty minutes. David began telling me about the Maasai who lived on the plains.

"They are very different from the Maasai who live in the highlands. We have allowed ourselves to be influenced by white people and have taken up some kinds of technology. In contrast the traditional Maasai people in the plains have refused to be influenced by white people and live by the old ways. The plains people can't rely on a crop for a good harvest so they rely on animals. They are herdsmen."

When the car swung off the tarmac road I could only just make out the barest of worn pathways. Ahead of us lay a wide plain with a mountain in the distance.

"You see the mountain?" David pointed. "My sister lives near it."

We travelled the Loita Plain for one and a half hours, heading towards Endoinyo Narasha. The landscape was totally different now. The plain was flat and arid with patches of grass and shrubs of varying heights. No matter how far we drove, that mountain ahead seemed to stay exactly the same distance from us. It would have been very tedious had it not been for the animals. David's cousin Cyrus knew a lot about animals and identified many different kinds for me. To my surprise there were cattle, sheep and goats grazing amongst the wild animals. We saw wildebeest and thousands of zebras.

"They're common zebra," Cyrus told me, though I couldn't see any difference between them and other zebras I'd seen. They were all black and white and vaguely horse shaped.

I saw plenty of giraffes and started to get a bit snap happy with my camera.

"Are they gazelles?" I asked at one point and the driver helpfully stopped the car.

"Thomson gazelles there," replied Cyrus, "And Grant's gazelles further away."

"Isn't that a kampala?" I asked as another herd of deer-like animals moved into view.

The men with me burst into laughter.

"What have I said wrong?" I asked.

"They're impalas," chuckled Cyrus.

"Kampala's a sickness," David wiped his eyes.

I shrugged. "Well, I knew what I meant!" And took several photos of the impalas.

We drove a little further before we stopped again for more photos. This time it was mongooses, (or is it mongeese?!) and a tortoise that was just standing in the road. Later on we saw antelopes and I saw a buzzard circling and landing fairly near us. A hyena slunk away from the roadside, carrying something in its mouth.

The mountain in the distance still hadn't drawn any nearer to us when we saw a committee of vultures ahead on the road. They hopped away as we drove up, exposing the skeleton of an animal in the dust. They were large birds, very ugly and looked at us sideways, as if wondering whether one of us would make a nice meal. We got out of the car with the vultures flapping and hopping away from us and Cyrus examined the skeleton. The vultures had obviously nearly finished their meal.

"It was probably a wildebeest killed by a hyena," Cyrus pronounced as he bent down and picked up the tail.

"What are you going to do with that?" I asked as we got back in the car.

"Sell it to a tourist shop – it's a souvenir."

I shuddered but later on I saw racks of them in a gift shop. They cost more than they were worth! I took some photos of vultures before we drove away.

"Were they any particular kind of vultures?" I asked Cyrus.

"Yes, there were two kinds there," was his reply. "White-necked vultures and White-headed vultures."

At last we reached the traditional Maasai home and the mountain looked a little closer than it had done. As we drove up to the compound I could see that there were a series of low huts all joined together. At regular intervals there were openings in the walls and as we drew up outside the compound, people just appeared through these openings. We were greeted by David's sister and taken through to the compound.

"There are five families living here," David explained to me, "And they all belong to the same clan. Each opening in the wall indicates a family's home."

What struck me first was the amount of flies. There had been flies at David's house but the air had been cooler and fresher up there. Down here on the plain it felt quite stuffy. There was also a strong smell of animal dung. As we walked past the joined huts, I realised that they were constructed of mud and dung. Flies flew all around me and settled on the faces of the children around us. David was handing out a sweet to each child as a present. I wanted to wipe the flies off their faces but they didn't seem too concerned about them and just ate the sweets hungrily.

In the centre of the enclosure made by the huts was a circle of stakes with parts of bushes hanging from them. In the area inside the stakes were huge piles of cow and goat dung – the stench was overpowering and the sound of the flies filled my ears. David saw me looking at the stakes.

"The animals are driven in here at night," he told me. "Then bushes are woven between the stakes so that the animals can't get out. During the day the men take them away to graze. Let's go in now, shall we?"

He gestured to the nearest "doorway". I had to bend double to enter and breathed in hot air. The main room was quite small which explained the heat. To one side I saw another room.

"That's for the young animals," David explained as he followed me.

"The young animals?"

"The young ones stay in here overnight so that they don't feed from their mothers until their owners have taken the first milk."

David's sister gestured me to a stool and then busied herself preparing food for us. I ṣat down carefully on the low stool. It seemed be quite sturdy. A sudden high-pitched mewl nearly made me fall off. Down by my feet squatted a thin cat that meowed the whole time we were there. It was tethered by one foot to the stool and I wondered what it was kept for.

"It's very important for them to have the milk," David was explaining. "They mix the milk with blood and drink it."

I hoped I wouldn't be offered milk to drink. In the middle of the floor was a fire pit, which fortunately was unlit. David told me afterwards that the fire was only lit twice a day – once for breakfast and once again in the evening for supper. I noticed two bed-like objects on either side of the room made of hard mud and asked David what they were.

"They are the beds," he replied. "My sister sleeps on one with her daughters. Her husband sleeps on the other with their sons."

We spent the afternoon in the close confines of the hut and met David's sister's husband who was the chief of the tribe. The atmosphere was friendly and relaxed and we talked mostly about the Maasai culture and way of life. The Maasai there were very interested in Christianity in general but none of them had the desire to actually be a Christian.

Monday 3rd to Tuesday 4th May – Safari!

I was waiting in David's four-wheel drive in Narok whilst provisions were being obtained for my safari. There were only two days left before I had to return to England so I was feeling quite sad. On the other hand I was actually going on a mini safari for the first time in my life and I was really excited about all the animals I was going to see!

We had already picked up our cook – John – who lived in Narok and he was buying all the food we would need for two days. David had gone off to meet Pastor Andrew who was from

Tanzania and had spent the weekend ministering in Narok. The cook returned to the car laden with bundles of food at the same time David arrived with Pastor Andrew. I sat in the front with David, who drove. The food was packed in the boot with the luggage and Pastor Andrew and the cook John sat in the back. We were off! Just outside Narok we picked up David's cousin Cyrus. I was pleased to see him as he'd proved himself very informative already about animals and birds. I just wished he wouldn't keep referring to impalas and chuckling at me.

We followed the tarmac road out of Narok for a while and then turned off onto the wide plain. I thought we were nearly there and kept looking around me excitedly. We were dwarfed by the vista around us. The only tall objects on the plain were acacia trees and giraffes. We travelled a long while following a dirt track across this plain and saw wildebeests and impalas. (I did get the name right this time much to David and Cyrus' amusement!)

At length we arrived at a pair of wrought iron gates with fences stretching away on either side. Just before the gates were several huts offering gifts and food.

"Let's have lunch," suggested David. "I think it's still a way to go before we reach our lodge."

Feeling a bit frustrated as I just wanted to get in the safari park and see the animals, I reluctantly agreed. We parked the car and went into the hut that sold food. The place was filthy and stank of stale food and drink. My heart sank and my stomach rolled. David ordered us a rice dish and when it arrived the food was barely hot. I had a sinking feeling in my belly as I watched the men tuck into the meal with relish. What if the rice had been reheated? I knew of a friend back in England who had nearly died due to rice being improperly reheated. I frowned at the food wondering why I was feeling so negative about it. Silently I prayed over the meal asking God to protect us all from food poisoning. I managed to eat the rice, and once I had finished we left the hut.

As we drove through the gates into the Maasai Mara National Reserve, all thoughts of food poisoning vanished from my mind. I was here – on safari! I looked around excitedly and saw only long, green grass ranging in every direction.

"It's the rainy season," Cyrus commented, noticing my frantic searching of the horizon for an animal. "That's why the grass is long. It's good camouflage."

I was not impressed. I wanted to see wild animals!

"Also, it's the hottest part of the day now, they're all asleep," he mentioned.

Oh well, I thought, *I've only just got here*. It was fifteen miles to Tarek Lodge by the Tarek River. At one point Cyrus pointed out an elephant in the distance. But he must have had sharp eyes because I couldn't see anything at all expect the long grass rustling as we passed. As we drew near the Tarek River however we saw more impalas and some warthogs.

"Oh look!" I cried, seeing another of the funny looking beasts. "Another water hog!"

Cyrus started laughing.

"What have I said wrong now?" I asked indignantly. "It's a water hog isn't it?"

"No Monica," replied Cyrus trying to control his laughter. "It's a warthog."

And just to make me feel at home I saw several giraffes as we neared Tarek Lodge. Not far from the Lodge was a stretch of that fencing again with a pair of familiar wrought iron gates. Another entrance to the park I deduced. As we carried our luggage into the Lodge I was feeling a bit disappointed, wondering if I'd actually see anything different from the animals I'd seen on the way here.

Tarek Lodge was self-catering and by taking this lodge we each saved £100 a day. Instead, the hire of the lodge cost us only £5 each. Of course we had to pay John, our cook, but he was still cheaper than the reserve's own caterers. Apparently John did this kind of thing quite often. He had been to the reserve many times and didn't go out to see any animals. Instead he stayed at the lodge and prepared all the meals.

We had a room each with en suite facilities – cement floors in the toilets instead of earth, and cold showers. I liked my room – it smelt clean and dry. As I unpacked I enjoyed the sound of the river running past, very close to the Lodge.

At 4.00 pm we set out again, David driving and me with my camera. Cyrus and Pastor Andrew sat in the back, with Cyrus providing a running commentary on the animals we saw. The first creatures we saw were silver-backed jackals. Unfortunately we couldn't get close enough for me to photograph them but I got a good look at the five of them. Next we found hyenas carrying dead animals in their mouths. I watched them as they slunk away from our vehicle and managed to take a couple of photos. They were a lot bigger close up than I had expected. Their coats were really quite woolly too which I hadn't imagined they would be. As we drove along we flushed some animals out of the grass and it was exciting to be chasing them! The light was beginning to fade however and so we returned to Tarek Lodge for supper.

John had prepared a top class meal for us. It was like eating at a really posh hotel and there was far more food than any of us could eat. The meal was laid out ready for us underneath the veranda and we watched the moon rise as we ate. First there was a homemade soup as a starter. The main course was vegetarian as John had taken into account my aversion to meat whilst abroad. The sauces that accompanied the vegetarian dishes were superb. And to finish off we had fresh fruit. I was just getting nice and relaxed when David announced it was bedtime.

"But it's only 8.30 pm!" I protested.

"Yes I know," he said. "But we need to be up at 6.00 am for breakfast."

"The earlier we leave the house," Cyrus told me, "the more likely we'll see the animals. They all feed at dawn."

That was enough to stop my protestations and I went to bed. As I lay there in the dark all I could hear was rushing water, endlessly pouring outside. I thought it strange as there'd been no clouds in the sky at suppertime. I felt a bit depressed again as I fell asleep, thinking that if it was raining, the ground would be dreadfully muddy.

When I woke in the morning and went outside to the veranda for breakfast I stared in surprise. There had been no rain in the night, the sky was clear and the river was in full flow. I felt stupid. Of course, it had been the river I had heard and not rain. The sun came up as we ate breakfast and the day promised to be bright.

"What animals do you really want to see?" Cyrus asked me as we finished eating.

"Oh . . . Elephants!" I replied. "Hippos, cheetahs and leopards. Well, anything really!"

I felt excited again as we set off. I clutched my camera like a child and stared into the long grass almost willing the animals to step out and be photographed. The first animals we saw were elephants and I managed to take a lot of photos. This wasn't due to my photographic skill though. The elephants moved really slowly and they were walking together as a herd parallel to the road we were following. I even managed to get photos of the babies.

"Can I get out and photograph them?" I wanted to know.

"No," said David firmly, shaking his head. "They're wild animals Monica, not zoo animals.

I contented myself with a few more photos as we drove round in front of the herd and left the road.

"There are more elephants in those trees ahead," Cyrus said quietly. "We could probably get quite close to them."

These elephants were moving very slowly through the trees, ears flapping occasionally, and their great feet treading carefully on the ground. When I thought I'd got enough photos of elephants, we drove on. On re-joining the

Elephants crossing the road on the Maasai Mara

road I saw some tawny colour beasts crossing the track ahead of us.

"Lions!" said Cyrus from the back seat.

I fumbled with my camera, but by the time I was looking through the viewer the lions had disappeared into the long grass. A short while later Cyrus told David to slow down and pointed out several shapes asleep at the edge of the road, half hidden in the grass. To my delight the pride of lions was quite clear and I took several photos of them. (When I got them developed however, all I could see were several brown splodges amongst the grass.)

The road took us near the river again and we stopped to see the hippos playing. I couldn't get very good photos of them as they just popped their heads up out of the water, had a quick look round and then dived down again.

"Round the corner," I heard Cyrus saying to David, "Is where the rhinos congregate."

I pricked up my ears at this and David drove off the road moving closer to the river. The further we went the worse the

Stuck on the Maasai Mara

ground became. When we came in sight of the rhinos by the river the vehicle was slipping and sliding around, even with the four-wheel drive on. We weren't the only ones trying to see the rhinos and all the other visitors' vehicles were slipping around too. So I got to see rhinos from a distance, which was probably safer than being too close to them. David eased the vehicle back from the mud and we turned round to find the road again.

As we drove along I saw a sight that I really hadn't expected to see in Kenya. A low-flying hot air balloon sailed slowly, but gracefully ahead of us, the basket full of white people with binoculars and video cameras.

"A hot air balloon? Here?" I asked.

"Oh yes," David said. "Some lodgers get the reserve to organise hot air balloon trips for them at dawn so that they can see the park and the animals from the air."

"How much does it cost?" I wondered.

"Between £400 and £500," David smiled. "Did you want to go up in one of them?"

"No way!" I said firmly. "You surely can't see the animals very well can you?"

David shrugged.

"I much prefer being down here," I said. "I wouldn't have got very good pictures of the elephants from up there!"

When we got back to the road, David parked the vehicle and announced it was lunchtime. Only then did I realise how hungry I was and looked around hopefully for some food. John had provided a huge lunch for us. There were different kinds of sandwiches and even hard-boiled eggs. I felt I was in England, rather than Kenya. And for pudding there was a fresh pineapple. John had packed us a chopping board and knife and David chopped the fruit up and divided it between us. I was impressed at the efficiency and organisation. I was so used to the women in Kenya doing all the food preparation that I hadn't realised the men could prepare and serve food as well. I could have offered to help but I knew they would be insulted as I was their guest. I wondered how early John had had to get up in order to prepare this as well as our breakfast!

The heat was intense when we finished lunch and David took us back to the lodge for a rest. I think the men rested but I couldn't settle. I only had one more chance this evening to see some more animals. And then tomorrow I would be flying home.

We went out again at 4.00 pm and David drove in a different direction, looking for cheetahs and leopards. Although we saw many lovely birds, which Cyrus identified for us, we didn't see any big cats. As evening drew on and we made our way back to the Lodge, David saw five Maasai men driving herds of cattle off the Maasai Mara back to their homes.

"They've been grazing their cattle illegally!" David snorted and put his foot down on the accelerator.

At the sound of the vehicle rushing towards them, the Maasai men abandoned their herds and ran away. David chuckled grimly as we drove past the placid herds.

"Why did they run away?" I asked.

"They thought we were the Maasai police," he replied.

"What would have happened if we had been the police?"

"They'd have been whipped if the police were quick enough to catch them."

David glanced in the rear view mirror. "They're coming back now to their cattle. They won't graze on the Maasai Mara for a while!"

I found the Maasai sense of humour odd. David had no particular grudge against the men grazing their herds in the reserve, but it was illegal. We forded the river and drove back to the lodge actually driving outside the reserve. We passed many herds of cattle being driven home and to each one, David asked the same question:

"Was it you we saw on the Mara?"

I could hear he was only teasing but every herder looked scared and hurried his cattle away from us. As we came in through the gates near Tarek Lodge we saw baboons and zebras down by the water. I took my final pictures and then we went in for supper.

Leaving Kenya – Wednesday 5th May

The next morning we rose early and left the Maasai Mara as the sun threw long shadows across the tracks. It was a long drive back to Nairobi and we stopped in Narok to drop off Cyrus, John and Pastor Andrew. At last, seven hours after leaving Tarek Lodge, David and I arrived at the Mayfield Guest House in Nairobi. There we were met by Pastor Jack and Sylvester and I said goodbye to David. Jack and Sylvester took me back to Sylvester's house where Janet had prepared a meal for us. I wanted to ask again what had happened to Sylvester's wife, but Jack plied me with questions about my safari trip and I was kept busy telling them about all the animals I had seen.

Time seemed to be running through the hourglass faster than ever and after our meal, Jack and Sylvester took me to the airport in a taxi that, as usual, was late. We got to the airport just in time. I said a hasty goodbye to my hosts and dashed in to book my luggage and have my passport checked. Soon I was on the aeroplane and it taxied out onto the runway. I was pressed into my seat as the plane took off and saw the myriad lights of Nairobi flicker and burn in the darkness below. I blinked back tears, feeling that the five weeks had gone far too quickly.

Only this morning I had been in the Maasai Mara. Now I was on my way back to tame old England. My mind filled with pictures of the long grass waving in the breeze and of the river, rushing and gurgling past the lodge. I reflected on the wonder and beauty of nature, of the fierceness and gracefulness of the animals that I had seen. I could really appreciate now how nature worked together, how everything had a plan and that behind the plan was a Creator. Wherever I went I knew that God would be with me. If he could care for the wild things in the Mara, I knew that he would look after me too.

I also realised that through all my travelling to date I'd learnt that I didn't need to know the bigger picture God has in mind. All I had to do was be obedient to Him.

~ THE END ~